MIMESIS
INTERNATIONAL

HISTORY

n. 11

ANNA MARIA SCOGNAMIGLIO

CHESS MOVES IN THE ENERGY MARKET

West German Strategical Use of Energy Trade with the East during the Cold War

MIMESIS
INTERNATIONAL

© 2024 – Mimesis International
www.mimesisinternational.com
e-mail: info@mimesisinternational.com

Isbn: 9788869774799
Book series: *History,* n. 11

© MIM Edizioni Srl
P.I. C.F. 02419370305

TABLE OF CONTENTS

Simone Selva

FOREWORD

Since the end of the twentieth century a few studies on the financial relations between the western world and the Soviet empire before the end of WWII contributed to make sense of the complex economic and political bonds between the would be major players of the Cold War: from Soviet dependence on French financial assistance up to the outbreak of the Bolshevik revolution through to America's intervention to stem the ascendancy of Bolshevism by means of economic assistance[1], a cohort of well-established studies contributed to add new perspectives to scholarship on the relationships between industrial modernization and economic growth on the one side, and international finance on the other. This literature advanced knowledge about the economic relations between the United States and the old continent otherwise pivoted on the ability of West European and American banks to flock money from the old continent to finance America's most critical industrial take off at the end of the nineteenth century, and the reverse process of raising funds in industrial America to prop up the Allies in their effort during WWI and to finance most-wanted stabilisation policies across Western Europe before the beginning of the 1929

---

1   David S. Foglesong, *America's secret war against Bolshevism : U. S. intervention in the Russian Civil War, 1917-1920.* Chapel Hill : University of North Carolina Press, 1995; Jennifer Siegel, *For Peace and Money: French and British Finance in the Service of Tsars and Commissars.* New York: Oxford University Press, 2014; Kim Oosterlinck, *Hope Springs Eternal: French Bondholders and the Repudiation of Russian Sovereign Debt.* New Haven, CT: Yale University Press, 2016; H. Malik, *Bankers and Bolsheviks: International Finance and the Russian Revolution.* Princeton: Princeton University Press, 2018.

great slump, two research trajectories for long on top of the agenda of historians of international economic relations. These fresh new studies on East-West banking and financial relations greatly added to the history of international economic relations otherwise strictly tied to its transatlantic dimension.

As a matter of fact, for decades the historiography on international economic relations since the end of WWII has largely overlooked such East-West dimension in capital movements and economic diplomacy. The Soviet Union's refusal to get economic assistance from the European Recovery Program, as well as its seclusion from the new architecture of Bretton Woods, certainly help making sense of this black hole on the research agenda of economic historians of international relations: in fact generations of economic and financial historians were trained on the very foundation and further development of the Marshall Plan in Europe and Japan, as well as on its macroeconomic impact on the European and Asian economies. Likewise, research interests by both historians and international political economists on the global influence and impact of the economic institutions of Bretton Woods pushed the historical discourse all the way down in the same direction, crafting a tangle of reconstructions focused on the nations and economies touched by the Bretton Woods institutions and the regional development banks established after 1945. One more plausible explanation worth mentioning is the ideological dimension that shaped the cultural debate on the origins of the Cold War before the end of WWII: whether animated by Soviet-friendly western intellectuals or U.S.-centered interpretations, such debate contributed to trace a line of separation between the western economies and the Soviet society at variance with any cultural environment ideal and fruitful to research the economic and financial relations between the two blocs during the Cold War. Notwithstanding this absence of relations between the Soviet universe and the western capitalist democracies from the agenda of economic and financial historians on the post-WWII decades, since the 1990s a number of authoritative scholarships on the economic

Cold War rose to prominence[2]. Based on the twin premise that the Cold War soon turned to be an economic race between the two blocs premised over embargo policies, mutual commercial and financial seclusions, and economic competition, this literature unveiled how industrial, trade and economic players on either side of the iron curtain repeatedly violated such set of embargo policies and overcame the economic and trade walls erected to divide vested economic interests on both sides. This literature presented three peculiarities: firstly it set economic and trade relations against the analytical framework of the Cold War: as such these cohort of economic bonds were reconstructed and portrayed as breaches and violations of the economic spheres of influence that arguably shaped the international economy during the Cold War[3]. In second instance by and large these studies focused attention on trade relations between the East and West in the age of industrial development and manufacturing, as such proving how they were premised over a conceptualisation of the Cold War as an industrial race between two advanced manufacturing systems[4].

In third instance this historiography pivoted on the powerful U.S. business and diplomatic influence on European attempts to overcome embargo policies, thus making the economic Cold War one more out of many episodes of a history revolving around the American presence in the old continent and influence on Europe[5].

---

2   Michael Mastanduno, *Economic Containment: CoCom and the Politics of East-West Trade*. Ithaca: Cornell University Press, 1992.

3   Jan Jackson, *The Economic Cold War. America, Britain and East-West Trade, 1948-1963*. New York: Palgrave 2001; Jari Eloranta and Jari Ojala, eds. *East-West Trade and the Cold War*. Jyväskylä, Finland: Jyväskylä University Printing House, 2005.

4   Gertrude Enderle Burcel, Piotr Franaszek, Dieter Stiefel, and Alice Teichova (eds.), *Gaps in the Iron Curtain: Economic Relations between Neutral and Socialist Countries in Cold War Europe*. Krakow: Jagiellonian University Press, 2009.

5   Frank Cain, *Economic Statecraft during the Cold War : European Responses to the U.S. Trade Embargo*. London-New York: Routledge, 2007. Diane Kunz, *Butter and Guns. America's Cold War Economic Diplomacy*. New York: Free Press, 1997; Daniel Berger, William Easterly, Nathan Nunn, Shanker Satyanath, "Commercial Imperialism? Political Influence and Trade During the Cold War", *American Economic Review*,103, 2, 2013, pp.863-896.

Therefore, this literature did not move away from an approach to the economic relations between the East and West premised over the idea that economic relations took place and shape in the framework of Cold War politics and U.S. trade embargo policies.

More recently, a fresh new wave of studies focused on the financial assistance provided by the Western world to the Soviet-dominated countries has moved away from this perspective by focussing on the role of private business and financial actors in propping up the Eastern European debt[6]. This literature has brought into the debate the complex relationship between international financial relations and energy diplomacy, nowadays a very popular topic on the research agenda of economic historians, by arguing that energy and finance, not the architecture of Bretton Woods, were the axes along which international economic relations between the two blocs mostly developed.

This first monograph by Dr. Anna Maria Scognamiglio comes along this way of reasoning and researching East-West economic relations with a focus on the economic relations between the Federal Republic of Germany and Eastern Europe during the Cold War through the case study of energy relations and trade in hydrocarbon compounds between Bonn and the Eastern bloc. Following suit the publication of studies by established scholars on the subject of German-Soviet relations in energy[7], the author tackles the history of economic diplomacy in the field of energy trade to make the argument that trading hydrocarbons not only was a step forward in the process leading up to Bonn's

---

6   Fritz Bartel, *The Triumph of Broken Promises. The End of the Cold War and the Rise of Neoliberalism*. Cambridge, MA: Harvard University Press, 2022; Stephen Kotkin, "The Kiss of Debt: The East Bloc Goes Borrowing", in Niall Ferguson, Charles S. Maier, Erez Manela, Daniel J. Sargent (eds.), *The Shock of the Global. The 1970s in Perspective*. Cambridge, MA: Harvard University Press, 2011; Daniela Gabor, *Central Banking and Financialization: A Romanian Account of how Eastern Europe Became Subprime*. Basingstoke: Palgrave Macmillan, 2011; Oscar Sanchez-Sibony, *The Soviet Union and the Construction of the Global Market. Energy and the Ascent of Finance in Cold War Europe 1964-1971*. Cambridge: Cambridge University Press, 2023.

7   Stephen Gross, *Energy and Power. Germany in the Age of Oil, Atoms, and Climate Change*. Oxford : Oxford University Press, 2023.

independence from the Western world and let the FRG safeguard German diplomatic relations with Moscow during the coldest years of the bipolar confrontation. Rather, a special relationship in oil and hydrocarbons contributed to the German rise to prominence in European politics and economics since the late 1960s. In particular, through a chronological reconstruction of the economic diplomatic relations between Bonn and Moscow from the 1960s through the 1970s and early 1980s focused on energy trade agreements and agreements on the construction of transnational energy infrastructures, the author argues that Bonn made progress on its way to increase the influence of West Germany on the GDR, and vitally contributed to push German foreign policy along the long route to *Ostpolitik*. After a general historical fine-tuning on the economic relations between Moscow and Germany in the twentieth century, the second section of this first-monograph study is devoted to make sense of the divergence, under the leadership of Konrad Adenauer, between a strictly U.S.-oriented West German foreign policy during the 1950s and 1960s, and an active German business community that since the early 1950s went all the way down to establish long-term commercial relations with the Soviet counterparts: the author meaningfully stresses how, notwithstanding Adenauer's opposition to an East-bound foreign economic policy, by the start of the 1960s the FRG had become the largest western exporter to the USSR. Therefore, the construction of a supra-national economic role by the FRG rested on a fundamental contribution by the West German business community, confirming the centrality of business interests and circles to the shaping of transatlantic economic and financial diplomacy in the twentieth century, a widely established historical interpretation[8].

A third section offers a reconstruction of the ways in which, under Brandt and Schmidt, the German business community and the FRG's foreign policy coalesced in making steps further on the way to erect and consolidate a foreign trade and industrial

---

8   Volker R. Berghahn, *American Big Business in Britain and Germany: A Comparative History of Two "Special Relationships" in the 20th Century.* Princeton, N.J.: Princeton University Press, 2014.

policy with the USSR pivoted on international energy relations autonomous from Washington and its western allies. In making this argument this section revives outdated studies on the strikingly diverging interests and foreign trade policies toward the Soviet world that supposedly divided Washington from Bonn during the Cold War[9]. The political-level pursuit of *Ospolitik* paired with an *Osthandel* policy, according to the author, even when, at the start of the 1980s, the Reagan administration and the U.S.-influenced western community implemented a wave of trade restrictions and sanctions on western corporations "trading with the enemy". Making matters all the more interesting are the final considerations that Dr. Scognamiglio offers on the unexpected attitude by the new Kohl government to keep trading energy products and promoting investment-related business interests notwithstanding his Western-prone political inclination and closer ties with Washington.

Therefore, the reconstruction rounds off by the time Kohl came to power. Arguably one might stress that this periodisation overlaps with the powerful rise to prominence of the German Deutsche Mark as an international currency in world trade and financial transactions. A better understanding of which relationship did exist between the rise to global reach of the FRG in world trade, here exemplified by the energy sector, and the global monetary role garnered in the meantime by the German currency is all the more crucial to get a better understanding of the trajectories that led to restoring a global economic role for the FRG before reunification: the auspice is that in a foreseeable time this linkage between a restored German global economic role and the powerful ascendancy of its currency in world financial transactions can find a spot on the research agenda of the economic and monetary historians of twentieth history's FRG and unified Germany.

In addition to a tidy archival and statistical reconstruction, the principal merit of this study is certainly that of locking the history

---

9   Hélène Seppain, *Contrasting U.S. and German Attitudes to Soviet Trade, 1917-91: Politics by Economic Means.* New York, N.Y. : St. Martin's Press, 1992.

of economic and trade relations between the FRG and the Soviet universe into the broader framework of Cold War economics and politics, instead of tracing a blurry line of separation as done for long in the extant literature on the subject.

In fact, through her reconstruction the author usefully contribute to detangle the history of the economic Cold War from an interpretation that has so far linked East-West trade to U.S. trade and embargo policies. This turns out to be clear all the more so if one consider that the role of U.S. foreign policy and that of U.S. energy corporations with a global reach powerfully shaped the system of international economic relations since WWII.

In conclusion, the history chronicled in these pages sheds a new light on the role of international energy relations in Cold War politics and economics: the FRG, for long under the tutorship of the Western world, made use of trade exchanges and industrial partnership in this field to accelerate its road to independence from Washington and to restore its global economic prominence.

To my Families:
my family by blood and my family by heart

GRAPHS

TABLES

ARCHIVES AND ABBREVIATIONS

BArch	Bundesarchiv
BDI	Bundesverband der Deutschen Industrie
BStU	Bundesarchiv – Stasi Unterlagen Archiv
CDU	Christlich Demokratische Union Deutschlands
CMEA	Council for Mutual Economic Assistance
CoCom	Coordinating Committee for Multilateral Export Controls
CSCE	Conference on Security and Cooperation in Europe
FRG	Federal Republic of Germany
GDR	German Democratic Republic
IGAT II	Iran Gas Trunkline II
NATO	North Atlantic Treaty Organization
NG (LNG)	Natural Gas (Liquefied Natural Gas)
OPEC	Organization of the Petroleum Exporting Countries
OSCE	Organization for Security and Co-operation in Europe
PA AA	Politisches Archiv für Auswärtigen Amt
SNGP	Soviet Natural Gas Pipeline
SPD	Sozialistische Partei Deutschlands
USA	United States of America
USSR	Union of Soviet Socialistic Republic

INTRODUCTION

The debate on the dependence of Germany, and all European states in general, on Russian energy supplies has intensified and broadened in recent years, due to both a political debate on energy transition and ecology, and as a result of more sensitive political and energy security issues following various crises occurred as a consequence of disputes between Russia and Ukraine since 2006.[1] This situation prompts the question of why Germany has become the European largest importer of energy from Russia, and how much and why it has suffered and continues to struggle with the consequences of the Russian supply cut that was implemented following the Russian aggression in Ukraine, which has been ongoing since February 2022.

This book presents a reconstruction of the economic and trade relations in hydrocarbons that existed between the Federal

---

1   For example: Justyna Maliszewska-Nienartowicz, 'Impact of Russia's Invasion of Ukraine on Renewable Energy Development in Germany and Italy', *Utilities Policy*, 87 (2024) <https://doi.org/10.1016/j.jup.2024.101731>; Vladivoslav B. Belov, 'A Paradigm Change in Energy Cooperation between Germany and Russia', *Herald of the Russian Academy of Sciences*, 92.Suppl 6 (2022), 512–20 <https://doi.org/10.1134/S1019331622120024>; Margarita Mercedes Balmaceda, *Russian Energy Chains: The Remaking of Technopolitics from Siberia to Ukraine to the European Union*, Woodrow Wilson Center Press Series (New York: Columbia University Press, 2021) <https://doi.org/10.7312/balm19748>; Odinn Melsted and Irene Pallua, 'The Historical Transition from Coal to Hydrocarbons: Previous Explanations and the Need for an Integrative Perspective', *Canadian Journal of History*, 53.3 (2018) <https://www.utpjournals.press/doi/full/10.3138/cjh.ach.53.3.03>; Stephen G. Gross, 'Making Space for Sanctions: The Economics of German Natural Gas Imports from Russia, 1982 and 2014 Compared', *German Politics and Society*, 34.3 (2016), 1–25.

Republic of Germany (FRG) and the Soviet Union (USSR) during the Cold War. It aims to answer the following questions: How did this exchange come about? Were the reasons purely economic or ideological? What role did the political and strategic dynamics between the blocs play in the establishment of this energy trade?

The fundamental premise of this analysis is that the trade of energy sources is inextricably linked to political, ideological, and economic considerations. Energy market trends have been driven by efficiency motivations, financial crises, social and institutional practices, and geopolitical dynamics.[2] As Stephen Gross notes, energy has always been and continues to be associated with every historical event, including crises as well as moments of growth. Consequently, historians must consider the role of energy in historical analysis, "identify thus actors who caused the emergence of high energy society, understand the rationale behind the actions, and explain why some individuals, organisations, and states revolted against this system."[3] This is particularly evident in the post-war period in Germany.

This book thus seeks to contribute to the growing awareness of post-war and Cold War history through the lens of energy between West Germany and the USSR. While the trade exchange between the two states has been studied (although most of the studies are now outdated), it is only in recent years that a new strand of research that gives energy its own unique and priority value within energy trade has emerged.[4] Rather than viewing

---

2   Stephen G. Gross, *Energy and Power: Germany in the Age of Oil, Atoms, and Climate Change*, Online edn (New York: Oxford University Press, 2023), pp. 7–8; Per Högselius, *Red Gas: Russia and the Origins of European Energy Dependence* (New York: Palgrave Macmillan, 2013), pp. 1–2.

3   Cit. Gross, *Energy and Power*, p. 6.

4   Gross, *Energy and Power*; Aurélie Bros, Tatiana Mitrova, and Kirsen Westphal, *German-Russian Gas Relations – A Special Relationship in Troubled Waters* (Berlin: SWP Research Paperà, 2017); Stephen G. Gross, 'The German Economy and East-Central Europe: The Development of Intra-Industry Trade from Ostpolitik to the Present"', *German Politics and Society*, 31.3 (2013), 83–105 <https://doi.org/10.3167/gps.2013.310305>; Werner D. Lippert, 'The Economics of "Ostpolitik": West Germany, the United States, and the Gas Pipeline Deal', in *The Strained Alliance. U.S. - European Relations from Nixon to Carter*, ed. by Matthias Schulz and Thomas A.

the energy sector as a mere backdrop to Germany's crises and developments, it aims to demonstrate its centrality to these crises and developments. The relevance of my analysis is contingent upon the mutual interests in the development of economic and diplomatic cooperation between West Germany and the USSR, extending beyond the energy sector to encompass the industrial one. Indeed, industrial companies too have been the driving force behind the expansion of energy trading over the decades.

The study has been shaped by a complex interplay of domestic, European and international dynamics, which have collectively influenced the evolution of energy policy at specific points in time. Although the work focuses on the mutually beneficial economic and political aspects of the renewal and extension of the Bonn–Moscow relationship, it highlights, thanks to a detailed analysis of archival documents, that energy agreements were used not only to maintain diplomatic relations between the two Blocs from the early 1950s onwards, with an increase from the 1970s onwards. The text emphasises the positive impact of this collaboration on the expansion of Germany's influence in Europe. In contrast, the United States have not been as influential in shaping European – particularly West-German – affairs since the 1980s, due to a number of points of divergence between the two countries' policies.[5]

This work is a revision of my Master's thesis and would not have been possible without the help and support of several people to whom I am deeply grateful.

Firstly, I also thank Prof. Simone Selva, who guided me in my research, supported me, and strongly believed in the potential of my work. I would also like to thank Prof. Stephen Gross, who kindly agreed to read my work as co-rapporteur in 2019, and Prof. Massimo Bucarelli for the insightful advice he provided, which has greatly enhanced the quality of the text.

Schwartz (Cambridge: Cambridge University Press, 2010), pp. 65–81; Alfred Jope, *Erdöl und Erdgas als wirtschaftliche und politische Faktoren* (Frankfurt a.M: Hirschgraben, 1976).

5   Helmut Schmidt, *Uomini al Potere* (Milano: Sugarco, 1987), pp. 128–29.

My gratitude also goes to the German archives staff and among those the staff of the Bundesarchiv in Koblenz. Not forgetting the contribution of Frau Barbara Groß, who welcomed and guided me in 2020 and in 2022. I would also like to thank all the staff of the Bundesarchiv-Berlin Lichterfelde, and archivists of the Stasi Unterlagen Archiv, especially Herr Lukas Flöttmann.

Outline of the book

The structure follows a chronological scan according to which two basic phases can be identified in the history of the Bonn Republic's foreign policy: one in the 1950s and 1960s, which was entirely in the spirit of Adenauer's integration with the West, and the other one from the early 1970s until the end of 1980s, which was shaped by Willy Brand's New Eastern Policy.[6]

The book is then divided into 3 sections.

The first section – "Before the FRG" – points out that the tradition of German-Soviet economic relations in the long 20th century began before the Great War and declined with the world conflicts.

After a brief historical perspective, the second section focuses on reopening of the market after WWII. It offers a reconstruction of Konrad Adenauer's push for greater cooperation with the West and a further disengagement from the East. The chapter describes how the FDR followed and supported American involvement in its foreign affairs under his leadership. Thus, it can be argued that the geopolitical tensions between Moscow and Washington at the time, especially during the period of McCarthyism and embargoes, concretely hampered Bonn's foreign trade. Within this context, however, German companies began to take private initiatives to access the Soviet market without government support. Indeed, this section shows how German business wanted to revive the flourishing tradition of cooperation to stimulate the

---

6   Karsten Rudolph, *Wirtschaftsdiplomatie im Kalten Krieg. Die Ostpolitik der westdeutschen Großindustrie 1945-1991* (Frankfurt a.M./New York: Campus, 2004), p. 273.

economy and make it autonomous from politics. For example, some West German businesspeople, despite US pressure, attended the Moscow Economic Conference in April 1952 and pushed for the creation of a German Committee for Economic Relations with Eastern Europe, whose main purposes were to improve and consolidate the presence of German companies in Eastern and Southeastern Europe, and to create a strong cooperation with the countries even in the absence of diplomacy. After these moves, the volume of German-Soviet trade was growing by the middle of the 1950s. The positive economic trend also resulted in the consolidation of West Germany's influential status on the European scene. In 1961, still under Adenauer's control, the FRG became by far the largest western exporter to the eastern bloc. In the following years, despite the delicate international situation and renewed national and transnational institutional attempts to limit trade relations with the USSR, especially in the energy sector with a strong pipe embargo, representatives of the German energy industry continued to sign bilateral agreements with the soviets. A balance between politics and economics was achieved only after the end of the embargo, with a political breakthrough: the resignation of Adenauer.

The following period, the new 'policy of movement' and then the *Ostpolitik* are described in the third section of the work. This strategy, in contrast to the earlier Adenauer's 'policy of strength' against the Eastern Bloc and German businessmen, based on cooperation between business, industry, and politics, changed the focus of politics and increasingly motivated a stronger cooperation with the countries of Eastern Europe. This section argues that the second phase of German foreign policy started with a closer work between politicians and businessmen in order to overcome the post-war crisis, to become more autonomous from the American control, to enhance their international prestige, and to gain greater room of manoeuvre in foreign trade with the East, both economically and politically. The study in this section advances historical knowledge about the management of the West German energy sector after the first energy shock. It highlights various contracts the West German companies entered into with Soviet hydrocarbon producers to support the new challenges. The analysis of these relations is particularly interesting when also compared with the American perception of the situation: in fact, the two Western allies reacted differently to the shock and its aftermath from the outset, and also viewed and treated the USSR differently. By the mid-1970s, therefore, the management of energy trade had become one of the key issues in the struggle for power in Europe between Washington and Bonn. The FRG officially became the exponent of a common European line of action in dealing with the second energy crisis. It extended and promoted cooperation with the USSR to other European countries, creating, in the early 1980s, a deeper dispute with the USA on the construction of the Urengoy gas pipeline.

1.
BEFORE THE FRG

The Federal Republic's path to becoming Russia's largest energy trading partner was long and arduous. It was shaped by the historical dynamics of trade between the two countries since the end of the nineteenth century.

A considerable volume of trade was already being conducted between the German and Russian Empires prior to the First World War. Globalisation had a profound impact on Imperial Germany's foreign trade in the late 1800s and early 1900s. The empire's principal trading partners during this period were Great Britain and the United States, followed by the Russian Empire and, finally, France.[1]

The First World War resulted in a disruption of domestic and foreign markets, which were only resumed at the conclusion of the conflict. The recovery process of trade relations has not been

---

[1] Prior to the commencement of the First World War, the Russian Empire constituted the second largest market of origin for imported products and the third largest destination market for exports. Data in Thomas Rahlf, *Deutschland in Daten. Zeitreihen Zur Historischen Statistik* (Bonn: Bundeszentrale für politische Bildung, 17 November 2022), pp. 294–95 <https://www.bpb.de/system/files/dokument_pdf/deutschland_in_daten_online_komplett.pdf>; Jürgen Sensch, 'Der Außenhandel Deutschlands. Basisdaten Für Den Zeitraum 1830 Bis 2000', 2009, tbl. ZA8358_C4b; ZA8358_C5b <https://doi.org/10.4232/1.8358>. Statistical data on the foreign trade of the German Empire from 1870 onwards can be used, but with caution. In fact, these data present a number of problems that cannot be overlooked when using them, including the different designation of regions of origin and destination over time and changes in methods of classifying goods. See Cornelius Torp, *The Challenges of Globalization*, Economy and Politics in Germany, 1860-1914 (Berghahn Books, 2014), pp. 13–19 <https://doi.org/10.1515/9781782385035>.

without its challenges. The post-war German economy suffered not only from the destruction of the conflict, but also from the heavy financial burden of reparations imposed on the defeated country by the Versailles peace. Concurrently, the Russian market was also experiencing a crisis: the economic system was undergoing a period of significant political upheaval, from the Revolution of 1917 to the formation of the USSR in 1922. This resulted in the dissolution of industrial stagnation, the erection of trade barriers, and the obstruction of traffic and trade.[2]

As observed by Harmut Pogge von Strandmann, the rehabilitation of German-Soviet economic relations after WWI constituted a pressing concern for German industrialists, which was addressed alongside military and foreign policy considerations. Their interest in re-establishing this trade contributed significantly to the evolution of German *Ostpolitik*, even before Brandt's Era and eventually led to the establishment of the "Rapallo Treaty".[3] It was signed in an hotel near Genoa in April 1922, during the World Economic Conference, by the Foreign Minister of the German Republic, Walther Rathenau, and the People's Commissar for Foreign Affairs in the Soviet Government, Gregory Chicherin.[4] Although Article 3 of the treaty provided for the resumption of diplomatic relations between the Weimar Republic and the Russian Soviet Federative Socialist Republic, the main purpose of ratification was to benefit from trade cooperation again. In Article 4, in fact, the reciprocal status

---

2   Carole Fink, Axel Frohn, and Jürgen Heideking, *Genoa, Rapallo, and European Reconstruction in 1922*, Publications of the German Historical Institute (Cambridge: Cambridge University Press, 1991), p. 6.

3   Harmut Pogge von Strandmann, 'Grossindustrie Und Rapallopolitik: Deutsch-Sowjetische Handelsbeziehungen in Der Weimarer Republik', Historische Zeitschrift, 222.1 (1976), 265–341 <https://doi.org/10.1524/hzhz.1976.222.jg.265>.

4   There is an extensive bibliography, mainly on the consequences of the Treaty of Rapallo. Others include Eva Ingeborg Fleischhauer, 'Rathenau in Rapallo: Eine notwendige Korrektur des Forschungsstandes', *Vierteljahrshefte für Zeitgeschichte*, 54.3 (2006), 365–415; Stephanie C. Salzmann, *Great Britain, Germany and the Soviet Union: Rapallo and after, 1922-1934*, Royal Historical Society Studies in History New (London: Boydell, 2002); Fink, Frohn, and Heideking.

of 'Most Favoured Nation' was granted, in order to gain more favourable conditions in trade and customs. Following this, in Article 5, the German desire to facilitate relations between private companies was made explicit.[5] The German delegation justified the signing of the treaty with Moscow by pointing out to the Western powers that, four years after the end of the war, they were still refusing to consider the needs and demands of the Germans. The treaty signed bilaterally at the Genoa Conference was therefore necessary for Germany, not because it wanted to distance itself from the Western powers, but primarily to safeguard its own interests.[6] Furthermore, the decision to engage with the East was also consistent with a German policy of balancing East and West, which was espoused by German Chancellor and Minister of Foreign Affairs, Gustav Stresemann, since 1923. He admitted, he used relations with the Soviet Union as a counterweight to maintain sufficient room for manoeuvre and secure German place in the order of European states.[7]

Such a cooperation was actually accepted by Western powers because it was not considered to be a big threat to their national security. Actually, while Germany enjoyed a favourable position with the USSR, Britain and the United States also remained close competitors in the Eastern market.[8]

Net of data, following the Rapallo Treaty, the Weimar Republic became the main trading and diplomatic partner of the USSR in the West.[9] The delicate balancing act continued in the following years, confirming West Germany's particular interest in the USSR. The "Treaty of Berlin", a treaty of friendship and neutrality signed on 26 April 1926, marked the confirmation of the alliance

---

5   Politisches Archiv des Auswärtigen Amtes (PA AA), RZ 101/28206, Rapallo Vertrag, fols. 33-34.
6   PA AA, RZ 101/28206, Reply of the German delegation to the statements of the 18th of April, 22 April 1922, fols. 127-130.
7   Salzmann, p. 322; Klaus Hildebrand, *Das Vergangene Reich*, Deutsche Außenpolitik von Bismarck Bis Hitler 1871-1945. Studienausgabe (Oldenbourg Wissenschaftsverlag, 2008), p. 459 <https://doi.org/10.1524/9783486719352>.
8   Salzmann, p. 102.
9   Rudolph, p. 12.

between Germany and the Soviet Union and the willingness to reinforce it. This pact had a strong political significance, as it represented a strengthening of German-Soviet international relations following the Locarno Conference. However, it also had a strategic character in the economic sphere, as it ensured a credit to the Soviet Union, which was experiencing a severe economic crisis, in order to strengthen the Russian foreign trade capacity to the pre-war volume and consequently consolidate Germany's international position.[10]

The signing of the Treaties of Rapallo and Berlin led to a real improvement in trade between the Weimar Republic and what had become the Soviet Union. Although the volume of exchanges did not reach pre-war levels, as hoped, there was an improvement after the war already in 1925. In 1913, the German market accounted for 29.9% of all products imported to Russia and received 47.5% of all Russian exports. In 1929, the share of the Soviet Union in German statistics on export and import reached 23.3% and 22.6% respectively. By 1932, however, the share of imports had fallen to 17.5%, while soviet exports to the Weimar Republic had almost reached pre-war levels, accounting for 46.5% of all products imported in Germany.[11] Specularly, the relative share of other Western supply partners declined.[12] The majority of the goods imported from the Soviet Union during the period between the two world wars were raw and semi-finished materials, agricultural products and foodstuffs. Only a portion of these imports were already energy fuels, such as crude oil.[13] Indeed, the Soviet Union established *Sojusnefteexport*, the first national oil company, only in 1922. This company became a potential adversary for Western and American oil companies

---

10   von Strandmann, p. 322.
11   Bernd Höpfner, 'Der Deutsche Außenhandel 1900 – 1945.', 2011, p. ZA8469_B310, Published: GESIS Datenarchiv, Köln. ZA8469 Datenfile Version 1.0.0, <https://doi.org/10.4232/1.10317>.
12   Rahlf, p. 291.
13   Aleksey Sorokin, 'The Soviet Union's Economic Relations with Austria and the Federal Republic of Germany: Political Factors and the Art of Diplomacy (1955-1964)', *Quaestio Rossica*, 10.5 (2022), 1657–73 (p. 1661) <https://doi.org/10.15826/qr.2022.5.753>.

engaged in trade in Europe. Despite American apprehension, Moscow increased its collaboration with Western partners for projects on Soviet soil during the 1920s. By the end of the decade, 15% of oil imports into Western Europe were sourced from the Soviet Union, representing for 22% of German and 68% of Italian oil imports, when oil from other Eastern countries was also considered.[14] By 1924, the Soviet Union had overtaken Poland as Germany's oil exporter and was second only to the United States of America.

The death of Stresemann in 1929 and the ascension of the Nazi Party to power marked a period of fluctuating relations between the two states. As early as 1928-29, military and political relations between the two states began to deteriorate, partly as a result of the German desire to move closer to the West. According to Stephanie Salzmann, German officials admitted in unofficial communications that economic relations were also in trouble.[15] Apart from the ideological clash between the Nazis and the Communists, the rise of Hitler and the Polish question worsened relations on the Eastern Front, effectively nullifying the Treaties of Rapallo and Berlin,[16] and foreign trade suffered greatly. In 1934, German Minister for Economics Hjalmar Schacht proposed a new economic plan based on bilateralism and foreign exchange control, with the objective of increasing the amount of foreign currency. Furthermore, the relationship between Germany and Russia deteriorated further following the explicit German declaration of intent to establish a new trade area in Southern Europe.[17] The sudden and drastic drop in trade between what was Nazi Germany and the Soviet Union also meant a complete halt to oil imports from the East. While in 1933 oil imports (in millions of Reichsmark) from Russia accounted for just under 20% of the total, by 1938 the supplier country

---

14　Claudia Wörmann, *Osthandel Als Problem Der Atlantischen Allianz. Erfahrung Aus Dem Erdgas-Röhren-Geschäft Mit Der UdSSR*, Arbeitspapiere zur Internationalen Politik (Bonn: Europa Union, 1986), xxxviii, p. 27.

15　Salzmann, pp. 138–39.

16　*Ibid.*, chaps 10–11.

17　Rudolph, p. 13.

disappeared from the Nazi government's statistical assessments of imports into the so-called 'Altes Reichsgebiet'.[18]

Graph 1: Oil import in the Interwar Germany

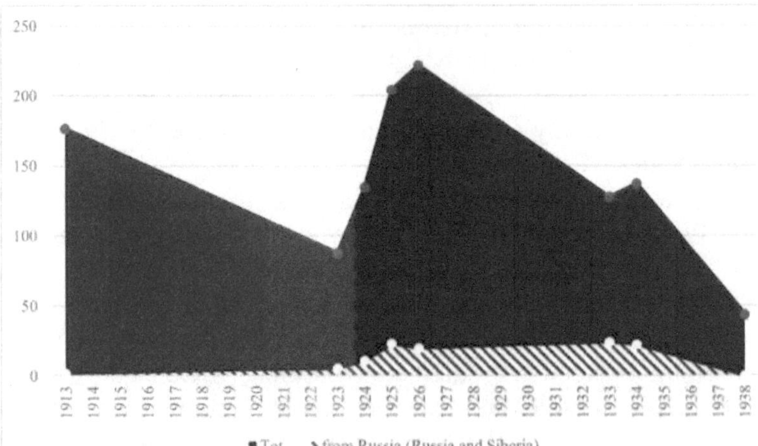

Source: 'Statistisches Jahrbuch für das Deutsche Reich', 1926, pp. 176, 184 <https://www.digizeitschriften.de/id/514401303_1924|log1>; 'Statistisches Jahrbuch für das Deutsche Reich', 1928, pp. 143, 159 <https://www. digizeitschriften.de/id/514401303_1927|log1>; 'Statistisches Jahrbuch für das Deutsche Reich', 1935, p. 204 <https://www.digizeitschriften.de/ id/514401303_1934|log1>; 'Statistisches Jahrbuch für das Deutsche Reich', 1940, pp. 273, 286 <https://www.digizeitschriften.de/id/514401303_1939|log1>.

In the aftermath of the Second World War, Germany was politically, economically, and socially devastated. The economic sector was experiencing structural difficulties, with food production and industrial output significantly below the levels observed a decade earlier. Additionally, the workforce was depleted, and price controls had been in place for several years. Comprising the four Allied powers, the Control Council for Germany was established, assuming supreme authority over

---

18   Data from 'Statistisches Jahrbuch für das Deutsche Reich', 1935, p. 204 <https://www.digizeitschriften.de/id/514401303_1934|log1>; 'Statistisches Jahrbuch für das Deutsche Reich', 1940, pp. 273; 286 <https://www. digizeitschriften.de/id/514401303_1939|log1>. Re-elaboration of the author.

various sectors of the defeated German state. At the same time, four zones of occupation were formed, where the victorious countries could manage the apparatus, including economy, in accordance with the directions decided in Yalta and Potsdam, but in an autonomous way.[19]

The approach of the victorious powers in their zones of influence and the restrictions of the Morgenthau Plan, which limited Germany's industrial production capacity, did nothing but throw an already devastated economy into chaos.[20] It soon became clear that the system had to be managed differently and that Germany's economic recovery was the key to Europe's economic recovery.[21] Among those called in the Western parts upon to reform the German economy was Ludwig Erhard. In 1947, Erhard joined the Administrative Council for Economics and became the director of the Bizonal Office of Economic Opportunity under the US zone military governor Lucius D. Clay and, a year after, the Director of Economic Affairs. Erhard was a supporter of the *Soziale Marktwirtschaft*, "social free market", also known as ordo-liberalism.[22] He proposed, in accordance with ordoliberal ideology, that Germany required a convergence of economic and social measures, including the implementation of a free market, a modest increase in income tax rates, legislative action to limit monopolies and foster competition. Additionally,

---

19   "Crimea (Yalta) Conference February 11, 1945" and "Report on the Tripartite Conference of Berlin (Potsdam Conference)" in *The Federal Republic of Germany and the German Democratic Republic in International Relations. Vol. I: Confrontation and Cooperation*, vol. 1, ed. by Günther Doeker and Jens A. Brückner, (Dobbs Ferry, NY: Oceana Publications, Inc., 1979), 13–25; 40–48.

20   Alan Bollard, 'A Continental Middle Way: Ludwig Erhard and Social Market Economists', in *Economists in the Cold War: How a Handful of Economists Fought the Battle of Ideas* (Oxford University Press, 2023), pp. 137–39 <https://doi.org/10.1093/oso/9780192887399.003.0004>.

21   Gustavo Corni, *Storia della Germania. Da Bismarck a Merkel* (Milano: Il Saggiatore, 1995), p. 291.

22   Gross, *Energy and Power*, pp. 48–52; Volker R. Berghahn, 'Ordoliberalism, Ludwig Erhard and West Germany's "Economic Basic Law"', *European Review of International Studies*, 2.3 (2015), 37–47; Werner Abelshauser, *Deutsche Wirtschaftsgeschichte. Von 1945 bis zur Gegenwart* (München: C.H.Beck, 2004), pp. 92–98.

he claimed the reorganization of the working and monetary sectors. However, as Stephen Gross points out, the ordoliberals did not place too much emphasis on the energy sector, but rather on agriculture and labour.[23] Erhard had flexibility and room for manoeuvre, but not completely: the pressures from Anglo-French authorities in part modified his plan, but nonetheless the Economist was able to de-nazify West-German economy in a relatively short period of time. He removed price, allocation, and rationing regulations, cut taxes, and created new jobs. Within a few years, industrial production and the German economy also recovered. There was a notable decline in absenteeism, with industrial production per capita exceeding three times the previous level. Furthermore, the re-establishment of money as the preferred medium of exchange for economic activity was evident, creating the so-called "German economic miracle".[24]

Erhard's approach to trade control policy was characterised by a high degree of strictness, particularly in relation to the USSR.[25] The currency reform implemented in the Bi-zone and the French zone, as well as in West Berlin resulted in intense conflict with the Soviet Union, like the Berlin Blockade, and the subsequent division of the territory into two states.[26]

---

23 Gross, *Energy and Power*, p. 51.

24 Bollard, pp. 140–45; Tamás Vonyó, *The Economic Consequences of the War: West Germany's Growth Miracle after 1945*, Cambridge Studies in Economic History (Cambridge: Cambridge University Press, 2018); Mark E. Spicka, *Selling the Economic Miracle: Economic Reconstruction and Politics in West Germany, 1949-1957*, Monographs in German History (New York: Berghahn Books, 2007), xviii.

25 Rudolph, p. 15.

26 Corni, p. 299.

Graph 2: Direction of German Exports 1928-1938-1948

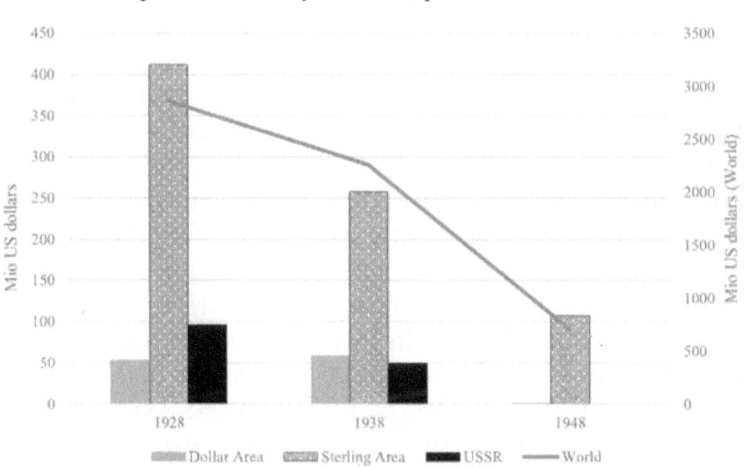

Source: 'International Trade Statistics 1900-1960' (United Nations Statistics Division (UNSD), 1962), tbl. XXV–2 <https://unstats.un.org/unsd/trade/imts/ Historical%20data%201900-1960.pdf> [last accessed 24 May 2024].

The situation only worsened after 1948.[27] The German economy has historically demonstrated a notable degree of independence from international trade. However, ideological issues and the zonal division of the post-war economy reduced the country's reliance on the global market. Prior to 1948, trade outside the borders of the zones was virtually non-existent, with the purchase of goods abroad being the exclusive prerogative of the occupying powers. The establishment of inter-zonal trade contracts was also not pursued (instead, the growth of the black market between the zones, particularly with the Soviet zone of influence, became the norm). Specifically, foreign trade was responsibility of the Allied Joint Export-Import Agency (JEIA),[28] – although each zone had its own office for foreign trade relations and initiated

---

27   Abelshauser, pp. 81–82.
28   JEIA: <https://images.library.wisc.edu/History/EFacs/GerRecon/Bizonal/ reference/history.bizonal.i0011.pdf>.

its first import-export relations after the war in 1946 – in the British-American Bi-zone and the Office du Commerce Exterieur (OFICOMEX) in the French zone, which focused on the import of foodstuffs.[29] The JEIA and the OFICOMEX have been established to further American, British and French interests and to guarantee a weak Germany for an extended period, in order to prevent the risk of a new war. At that time, the USA was implementing political measures with the objective of isolating Russia and communism, trying to safeguard 'national security' and prevent the country's descent into communism. For example, in 1949, they attempted to restrict the export of strategic materials, equipment and industrial products to the Soviet bloc nations with the Export Control Act.[30] And at the same time, despite the partial opening up of foreign trade, the JEIA did not allow the resumption of economic trade relations with the Soviet Union.[31]

In the wake of the Soviet blockade of Berlin and the subsequent occupation of Czechoslovakia, US President Harry Truman sought to exert control over the German economy and trade policy, as well as its international affairs. So, the American administration, with the support of other Western countries, sought to achieve a balance between economic and security interests through collective action in a multilateral export control regime known as the Coordinating Committee for Multilateral Export Controls (CoCom). The CoCom was designed to regulate the export of Western European goods, including industrial machinery for the exploration and production of petroleum, to Eastern countries.[32] Germany agreed to CoCom and became the testing ground for the American embargo policy against the

---

29   Abelshauser, pp. 83–84.
30   Michael Mastanduno, *Economic Containment: Cocom and the Politics of East-West Trade*, Cornell Studies in Political Economy (Ithaca, NY: Cornell University Press, 2019), p. 27; Wörmann, xxxviii, p. 8.
31   Bollard, pp. 145–46.
32   Mastanduno; Bernhard Grossfeld and Abbo Junker, *Das CoCom im Internationalen Wirtschaftsrecht, Das CoCom im Internationalen Wirtschaftsrecht UniMi* (Tubingen: J.C.B. Mohr, 1991).

Soviet Union in Europe.[33] The implementation of these trade measures resulted in a significant decline in German-Soviet economic relations, but also in a decline of German foreign trade revenues, particularly in trade relations with the West and the USA.[34]

---

33   Wörmann, xxxviii, p. 14.
34   Abelshauser, p. 63.

2.
FROM 1949 TO 1969

2.1 *Despite Adenauer's will*

Following the traumatic experience of National Socialism and the subsequent reluctance of the majority of citizens to engage in politics, the post-war period saw the dominance of the Christian Democratic Union (CDU), which became the leading political force within West Germany for more than a decade. Its ascent was facilitated by a greater political commitment, coupled with a development of successful administrative and economic unification within the Western territories. These factors led to the eventual acceptance of the possibility of a unified West German state.

Following a gestation period of approximately one year, on 15 September 1949, Konrad Adenauer, an exponent of the Bavarian sister party of the CDU, was elected as the first Chancellor of the new-born Federal Republic of Germany. In May of that year, the so-called *Grundgesetz*, a basic law which subsequently became the Constitution of the FRG was signed. Based on the new Constitution, the role of the president in the state management team was diminished, while the central decision-making figure was the chancellor, who became responsible for defining the binding guidelines for each ministry.

The foreign policy of the Adenauer government was West-oriented, forming the core of its agenda. The two cornerstones of his strategy were the refusal to engage in dialogue with East Germany and the support of a strong international position within the political and military West Alliance.[1] Konrad Adenauer's foreign policy can be described as a 'policy of strength', which was strongly oriented towards the USA and distrustful of the Eastern bloc.[2] One of the most pivotal decisions Adenauer made following his ascension to power was the signing of the Petersberg Agreement with the three Allied High Commissioners in November 1949. This agreement afforded the Federal Republic greater flexibility on the international stage.[3]

Adenauer, as the inaugural chancellor, was additionally tasked with overseeing the economic sector. However, this has increasingly been established on the basis of a political-ideological strategy, rather than an economic one. The recovery was sustained by the process of globalisation and the capacity to trade with varied and distant markets, like Latin America. Moreover, the business community was encouraged to invest in Western markets, while the focus on Eastern ones began to wane.[4] German foreign economy was, indeed, suffering the lack of trade relations with the Soviet Union and Eastern Powers. In fact, the import of natural goods, such as oil and coal, has been stopped after the WWII and never restored.[5]

The Petersberg Agreement enabled the Federal Republic to join the Council of Europe and the International Ruhr Agency as early as November 1949, and to be included in the Marshall Plan, which facilitated closer ties between the FRG with the USA. It was only after this affiliation that Germany was

---

1   Anthony Ian, *Arms Export Regulations*, in Ksenia Demidova, 'The Deal of the Century: The Reagan Administration and the Soviet Pipeline', in *European Integration and the Atlantic Community in the 1980s*, ed. by Kiran Klaus Patel and KennethEditors Weisbrode (Cambridge University Press, 2013), pp. 59–82 (p. 59).

2   Julia Von Dannenberg, *The Foundations of Ostpolitik: The Making of the Moscow Treaty between West Germany and the USSR*, Oxford Historical Monographs (Oxford: Oxford University press, 2008), p. 19; Corni, p. 306.

3   'Agreement Between the Allied High Commission in Germany and the West German Federal Republic, Signed at Bonn, November 24, 1949', *International Organization*, 4.1 (1950), 184–87.

4   Rudolph, p. 41.

5   Abelshauser, p. 84; Wörmann, xxxviii, p. 27.

permitted to initiate a "gradual re-establishment of consular and commercial relations with those countries where such relations appeared advantageous."[6], including the USSR, even though an official economic policy with the East did not exist before 1951. Furthermore, in October 1951, West Germany joined the General Agreement on Tariffs and Trade (GATT). Germany had historically been dependent on international markets, and the new acts and manoeuvres for opening Germany to the world were actually a crucial element in the reconstruction of the German economy. The Federal Republic was able to gradually recover from the negative trade balance and achieve a surplus in 1952.[7] Eventually it was entering in the International Capital Market.

Despite Adenauer's staunch support of *Westpolitik*, which entailed opposition to the Soviet Union and the rejection of a unified, neutral Germany, during his term in office, a pronounced inclination towards the East emerged, particularly within industrial and non-governmental realms. Actually, it soon became evident that the economic policy imposed by the USA on West Germany would not be beneficial in the long term. While the USA provided the necessary military aid and funds for the reconstruction of the FRG, the American domestic market did not open up to German goods. Washington did not actively participate in the German economy and did not address the German offer of finished goods. In this context, European institutions, such as the Economic Commission for Europe (ECE), and German industrial representatives continued to advocate for the expansion of West-East trade and the restoration of legal trade between Western European countries and Russia, which had consistently ever been a reliable market for German industrial products.[8] Another issues that continued to impede

---

6   'Protocol of the Agreements Reached between the Allied High Commissioners and the Chancellor of the German Federal Republic at the Petersberg (November 22, 1949)', in *Documents on Germany under Occupation* (London/New York: Oxford University Press, 1955), pp. 439–42 <https:// germanhistorydocs.ghi-dc.org/pdf/eng/Founding%208%20ENG.pdf> [last accessed 24 May 2024].

7   Rahlf, pp. 302–3.

8   Rudolph, p. 35.

the development of relations with Moscow, both in practice and in terms of institutional frameworks, was the question of West Berlin and its role and treatment in the negotiations between the states. In order to overcome this impasse, in 1951 the *Berliner Abkommen* (Berlin Agreement) was signed, which involved both East and West Berlin areas, and despite a few crises, remained uninterrupted until the end of the 1980s.

Adenauer's *Westpolitik* was unsuccessful in preventing trade with the Eastern Bloc. Given that the government was not officially engaged with this issue, businessmen assumed the initiative to engage with the USSR too. For instance, they participated in the Moscow Economic Conference of April 1952, despite pressure from the USA.[9] Consequently, in December of that year, Erhard, at the time Minister of Economics, and industrial associations established the *Ost-Ausschuss,* the German Committee on Eastern European Economic Relations, an official corporate association recognised by the Federal Government. Its primary objectives were to enhance the presence of German companies, particularly those in the iron and steel industry, and foster robust collaboration in Eastern and South-Eastern Europe, the USSR, China and Romania, even in absence of diplomatic relations.[10] Nevertheless, the German government continued to disregard the *Ost-Ausschuss*'s work as a matter of state interest. This apparent indifference for the *Ost-Ausschuss*'s activities may have been driven by a desire to prevent a rapprochement between West and East from overshadowing and undermining Adenauer's anti-communist policy. In order to discredit the *Ost-Ausschuss*, the government questioned its economic aims, its legitimacy and reliability. In contrast, it emphasised the importance of signed agreements with the West, particularly with the United Kingdom.[11]

---

9   Rudolph, p. 38.
10   Sorokin, p. 1662; Karl-Heinz Schlarp, 'Das Dilemma des westdeutschen Osthandels und die Entstehung des Ost-Ausschusses der deutschen Wirtschaft 1950-1952', *Vierteljahrshefte Für Zeitgeschichte*, 2 (1993), 223–76 (p. 261).
11   Rudolph, pp. 85–86.

After two years, the inaugural attempt at *Ostpolitik* was faltering. Nevertheless, the business community persisted in asserting that the USSR and Eastern Europe were of paramount importance for the German balance of trade and that the FRG must re-enter into commercial relations with them, just as other Western countries had improved their foreign trade with the East. Moreover, as we have seen in the first section, the business community could rely on historical data to confirm the vital importance of the Russian market for the German economy.

It is now worth discussing the ideological tenets of Alfred Müller-Armarck, the esteemed head of the Policy Department in the Federal Ministry for Economic Affairs under Ludwig Erhard. As well as being one of the most important thinkers of ordo-liberalism, Armarck was convinced that the success of the West German economy depended on reintroducing market dynamics into the system. What made his ideas most popular and influential was his campaigning among industrialists and businessmen.[12] It was of paramount importance to him to consider political factors in formulating economic measures with regard to the East, and one of these political objectives was the reunification of Germany. Armarck's strategy proposed that the government should sign an agreement guaranteeing more free trade and free relations between Bonn and East Berlin. Such a strategy would also raise the international prestige of Germany, which was one of the last Western countries not yet signing a commercial agreement with the USSR.[13]

In accordance with Armarck's proposal, Adenauer would set aside his personal political grievances against the GDR. This was entirely at odds with Adenauer's political convictions. Initially, there were openings with the GDR, which the chancellor had opposed. The fundamental reasons that made inter-German trade so crucial for both parties encompassed both political and economic considerations. From eastern point of view, the political perspective was primarily, as well as the intent to

---

12   Spicka, 18:34.
13   Rudolph, pp. 98–99.

maintain the relationship between East and West Berlin and to eventually gain international recognition as a German state. On the other side, the objective was to sustain a high volume of trade.[14] Furthermore, East Berlin would also play a role, albeit a secondary one in the energy negotiations (as transit country for petroleum and petroleum products).

However, the Chancellor was not interested in reunifying Germany or having relations with the GDR. Furthermore, the recognition could also facilitate the signing of deals between Moscow and the representatives of German industries, relations which bypassed the government itself and could discredit West German political authority. His objective was for the FRG to be recognised on the international stage as an official and important entity, the unique German entity both in West and in East. Following a series of openings that appeared to indicate a willingness on the part of Adenauer to engage in discussions with the Soviet government regarding the potential for economic and trade relations with Moscow in June 1955, it was announced in August of the same year that such agreements would not be concluded. The so-called "Erhard Memorandum" underscored that economic negotiations were contingent upon the resolution of political issues and the resolution of disputes between the parties, with a positive impact on West Germany.[15] At the same time, also the "Hallstein Doctrine" was launched. The doctrine was based on the political beliefs of the State Secretary at the Foreign Office Walter Hallstein.[16] It held that the FRG was the only legally constituted German state, in contrast to the GDR, which lacked official recognition. Consequently, Bonn chose not to maintain diplomatic relations with all countries, effectively acknowledging the GDR. In this manner, the pursuit of political

---

14	Staatsarchiv Bremen (StAB), 4.92/2 706, Bericht des Herrn Bundeswirtschaftsministers Dr. Erhard über den grundsätzlichen handelspolitischen Standpunkt der Bundesregierung zur Frage des Interzonenhandels vor dem Ausschuß für gesamtdeutsche Fragen des Deutschen Bundestages am 7.5.1953, fol. 4.
15	Sorokin, p. 1662.
16	Von Dannenberg, p. 19.

influence was deemed to be of greater importance than the resolution of economic or internal political issues.[17]

Net of the political and economic measures of Adenauer and the USA against the establishment of trade relations, the year 1955 proved to be a pivotal one in the consolidation of German-Russian economic relations, as well as in the political sphere.[18] This was largely due to the efforts of the Soviet Embassy in Bonn.[19] Private agreements led by representatives from the German business community, such as Otto Wolff von Amerongen, facilitated the establishment of a framework for future collaboration.[20] To the end of Marshall Plan and the scale down of the CoCom Embargo,[21] the volume of German exports to Russia was increasing exponentially, while the imports from Russia to West Germany were also growing. German exports to the Soviet Bloc included machinery, such as excavators and chemical plants, which Russia required for the restoration of its energy industry. In return, Bonn imported raw materials, such as oil, coal and manganese, from Moscow.[22] A mere year later, the trade balance with the USSR of the FRG had shifted to a positive position, as shown in Graph 3.

---

17 Schlarp, p. 223.
18 Sorokin, p. 1659.
19 Rudolph, p. 111.
20 Since 1955 he was the chairman of the German East-West Trade Committee. Sven Jüngerkes, *Diplomaten der Wirtschaft. Die Geschichte des Ost-Ausschusses der Deutschen Wirtschaft* (Osnabrück: Fibre, 2012), pp. 95–96.
21 As early as 1948-49, the US had drawn up lists of categories of goods and equipment that could not be traded with the East. For the restrictions to be effective, Western countries had to adopt them. However, as early as 1953, certain Western countries, including West Germany, were allowed to sell certain items. See Mastanduno, pp. 64–87.
22 Rudolph, p. 117; Wörmann, xxxviii, p. 28.

Graph 3: West-German import from and export to the USSR (In Mio DM)

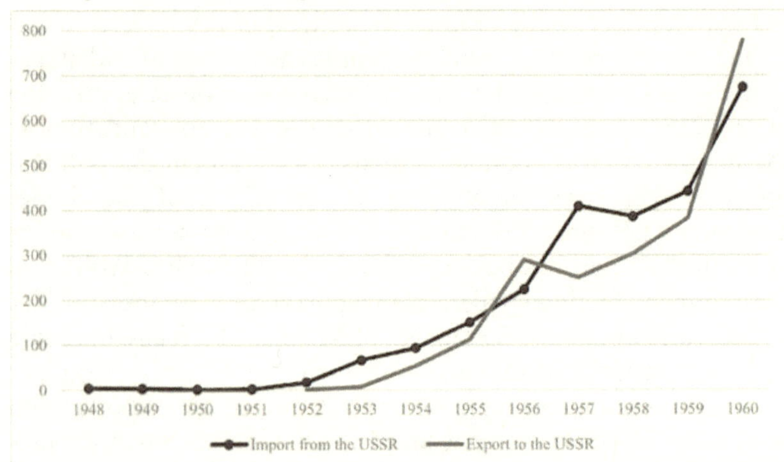

Source: Jürgen Sensch, 'Der Außenhandel Deutschlands. Basisdaten Für Den Zeitraum 1830 Bis 2000', 2009, tbl. ZA8358_C7 <https://doi.org/10.4232/1.8358>.

2.2 *Bridges towards East*

At the end of the '50s, a Committee for West-East Relations had been established and trade was on the rise. However, the direct diplomatic relationship between the German Federal Government and the Soviet Bloc was becoming increasingly strained. 1957 marked a pivotal year in the development of such relations.

In February 1957, the Soviet Prime Minister, Nikolai Bulganin, attempted to initiate a dialogue with Adenauer. The Chancellor was preparing for the election and viewed a rapprochement with the Soviet Bloc at that time as an opportunity to gain political appreciation and support.[23] He was aware that the *Bundestag* could approve a commercial treaty that would address one of the political issues inherent in his strategy: the facilitation of the repatriation of thousands of Germans residing in the USSR.

---

23   Rudolph, p. 121.

At the end of April 1958, Moscow and Bonn entered into an "Agreement on General Trade and Shipping Issues".[24] The agreement came in place for the exchange of machinery and equipment for raw materials and energy fuels, which would later become the cornerstone of the Bonn-Moscow trade. Bonn consented, moreover, to a limited most-favoured-nation clause in favour of Russia, in exchange for the required repatriation of such Germans.[25] Following CIA analysis, however, this agreement was little more than a declaration of interests, given that the Hallstein Doctrine remained in effect.

Even though the negotiations between the FRG and the USSR were still not considered to be solid and trustworthy, representatives of West German industry began taking part to Moscow fairs and, conversely, representatives of Eastern European countries, including the Soviet Union, began to be invited to Germany to the Frankfurt Fair as early as 1958-59.[26] Concurrently, Dwight Eisenhower, the new US President, agreed to liberalise the CoCom export control principles for Western Europe and remove the control list for large diameter pipes and other energy equipment. This facilitated an increase in German-Soviet trade in these commodities, which were used for the construction of energy infrastructure.[27] Over the course of some years, the general exchange of goods between Bonn and Moscow exhibited a consistent upward trend. At the beginning of 1959 imports from the USSR increased by almost 16%, with the share of direct imports rising from 52% in the first half of 1958 to 84% of total imports. Exports, on the other side, fell by 9%.[28]

---

24   Sorokin, p. 1662.
25   *"Western Europe: Economic Links with the Soviet Bloc". An Intelligence Assessment* (Directorate of Intelligence, 1 May 1983), p. 31 (p. 14), General CIA Records <https://www.cia.gov/readingroom/docs/CIA-RDP84S00555R000200050003-4.pdf>.
26   PA AA, B 41-REF IIA 4/ 18, Referat 704, fol.8; Referat 413, fol. 13.
27   Demidova, 'The Deal of the Century: The Reagan Administration and the Soviet Pipeline', p. 60.
28   PA AA, B 41-REF IIA 4/18, Ref. 704. Aufzeichnung. Osthandel der BRD im I. Halbjahr 1959, fol. 43.

Although the prevailing political tensions between the two blocs, including the Second Berlin Crisis and the construction of the Berlin Wall, it continued in the Sixties. The federal government and businessmen were at least attempting to distinguish between political and economic trade, *Osthandel* and Inter-German trade. In 1961, it was even decided that the non-political bilateral agreements suspended during the Second World War would have been reinstated.[29] In the same year, West Germany became the largest western exporter to the soviet bloc.[30]

2.2.1 *A Machiavellian game*

While energy had not been the main focus of the ordoliberals, it had become an increasingly important topic since the late 1950s.

At the beginning of the Fifties, coal was the primary energy source. Crude oil was not a significant contributor to the energy supply. The amount of natural gas used by the FRG was also minimal. The utilisation of coal declined significantly during the latter half of the 1950s, paving the way for oil to become the dominant energy fuel.[31]

The Suez Crisis of 1956 destabilised the world energy market and aggravated the coal crisis not only in the FRG but also in other countries around the world. It led Europe to ask more than a question about its energy policy and to consider how to stabilise the energy market and secure its energy position in the event of another crisis. One of the main issues that had to be tackled was Europe's

---

29 PA AA, B 41-REF IIA 4/19, Wiederhanwendung von bilateralen Vorkriegsverträgen, September 1961, fols. 48-58.

30 *Impact of Oil Exports from the Soviet Bloc* (Washington, DC: National Petroleum Council, 1964), p. 159 <https://www.energy.gov/sites/default/files/2022-11/1964-Impact_of_Oil_Exports_from_Soviet_Bloc-Supplement.pdf>.

31 Michael Farrenkopf, 'Short-Term Rise and Decades of Decline: German Hard Coal Mining after 1945', in *Boom - Crisis - Heritage: King Coal and the Energy Revolutions after 1945*, ed. by Lars Bluma, Michael Farrenkopf, and Torsten Meyer (Berlin, Boston: De Gruyter Oldenbourg, 2021), pp. 131–46 <https://doi.org/doi:10.1515/9783110729948-010>.

almost total dependence on a single source of fuel. Consequently, governments and international institutions advocated for a diversification of sources and suppliers. The transition from coal to other fuels in Europe, including the FRG, contributed to a shift in energy supply towards crude oil. In addition, natural gas too has emerged as a transitional and substitute fuel, gradually gaining traction in the German energy market.[32]

Indeed, following the coal crisis of 1958, West-German government began to question the maintenance of a constantly available and diversified pool of sources, recognising that energy was key to the development of a modern economy. One of the sources that began to be used more widely was oil, especially from the USSR.[33]

The shift from coal to oil and gas was striking in terms of its magnitude. In 1950, coal, both brown and hard, accounted for 88% of all energy consumption. By 1960, this figure had declined to 74.5%, and by 1970, it had fallen to 38%. Concurrently, the percentage of petroleum usage increased by approximately 10.4 times over the same period, while the consumption ranking of natural gas increased by 88.5 times in 1970 compared to 1950.

However, when viewed in absolute terms, the trend was different. In 1965, the diversification of primary energy use was markedly different from what is observed in 1960. Oil consumption increased by less than 1.5 times, reaching 40.92% of the total, while both types of coal decreased. At the same time, the percentage of natural gas consumption already did not exceed 1.25%. Oil became the most favoured fuel, accounting for 53% of all German energy consumption in 1970, while natural gas accounted for only 5.4% of German energy requirements.[34]

It is also of interest to examine not only the growth in expenditure on energy sources but also the supply markets. In 1960, West

---

32   Jope, p. 38.

33   Gross, *Energy and Power*, p. 47.

34   'Struktur des Energieverbrauchs' (AGEB - AG Energiebilanzen e.V., 2010), Zeitreihen bis 1989 <https://ag-energiebilanzen.de/daten-und-fakten/zeitreihen-bis-1989/>.

Germany accounted for 90% of its energy consumption.[35] However, the country produced only 19.2% of crude oil, with the remaining 80.8% imported particularly from the Middle East (64.7%) and the Caribbean (9.8%). Russia was the sole exporter of crude oil from the Eastern Bloc to the FRG, but the quantity exported was minimal, at approximately 4%.[36] There were actually many difficulties and incompatibilities between the parties in the rules and negotiations for energy trade, such as the different time limits to be imposed on contracts. But the need to open the German market to Soviet products also helped to overcome the negotiating obstacles.[37] Despite that, West Germany became in 1962 the largest importer of Soviet petroleum in Europe, ranking second only to Italy.

Graph 4: Total Soviet Bloc Petroleum Exports to Free Europe (NATO Members) by Country of Destination 1962 – thousand BBLS. per day

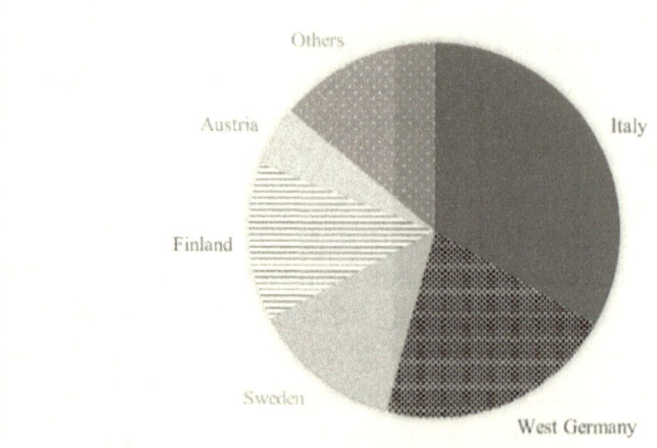

Source: Impact of Oil Exports from the Soviet Bloc (Washington, DC: National Petroleum Council, 1964), p. 31 <https://www.energy.gov/sites/default/files/2022-11/1964-Impact_of_Oil_Exports_from_Soviet_Bloc-Supplement.pdf>.

---

35   BArch Koblenz, B 102/163897, Report of Deutsches Institut für Wirtschaftsforshung, "Bedeutung und Möglichkeiten des Ost-West-Handels mit Energieröhstoffen", March 1973.

36   Data from Bundesamt für gewerbliche Wirtschaft, quoted by Frank Blom, *Beschaffungsmarktforschung* (Wiesbaden: Gabler, 1982), p. 161.

37   PA AA, B 41-REF IIA 4/18, Aufzeichung über den Stand der deutsch-sowjetischen Wirtschaftsverhandlungen, 1 December 1960, fol. 106.

First primary sources were a key strategic asset for the USSR. Brezhnev was aware that the exploitation of Russia's oil and gas resources could provide a solution to a number of domestic issues. Firstly, the sale of these resources could generate significant revenue of hard currency to improve the living conditions of the Soviet people and the payment of Western technology and know-how. Soviet industry was, indeed, unable to produce sufficient quantities of steel pipes, especially large diameter pipes, and so imported them from West Germany, Italy and Sweden, which were also the main oil importers. Secondly, the involvement of the USSR in the world energy market would enhance its global influence.[38] From 1956 onwards, the first of these objectives began to become a reality. In that year, German exports of large pipes to the Soviet Bloc resumed. Also in 1958, these special tubes were removed from the list of products embargoed by the West to the USSR, further boosting this trade.[39] At the time, approximately 60 to 90% of the exports from Western Europe to the Eastern Bloc consisted of foodstuffs, metals, machinery, manufactured goods and, above all, transportation equipment such as pipelines. Western Europe itself required the export of pipes not only because it made a significant contribution to GDP growth, but also because the USSR could build new pipelines to the West in order to increase oil and gas supply. An efficient transport network from the USSR to Europe was actually of paramount importance for the European energy supply, particularly for Germany, due to the continent's limited natural resources.[40] Over a period of about 4 years, from 1958 to 1962, the length of Soviet oil and gas pipelines exhibited a growth rate of approximately 80%.[41]

---

38 Charles William Carter, 'The Importance of Osthandel: West German-Soviet Trade and the End of the Cold War, 1969-1991' (The Ohio State University, 2012), pp. 35–36 <https://etd.ohiolink.edu/acprod/odb_etd/ws/send_file/sen d?accession=osu1346850432&disposition=inline>.
39 *Impact of Oil Exports from the Soviet Bloc*, p. 93.
40 *Ibid.*, p. 159.
41 *Ibid.*, p. 89.

Moreover, the pipes trade had a secondary economic advantage for West Germany itself. As purchaser and supplier of goods and equipment, indeed, Bonn could benefit from a discounted price on crude oil price. On the contrary the Satellite nations paid substantially higher prices for both crude oil and oil products. From 1955 to 1962 the average f.o.b.[42] export prices for Soviet crude oil to Free World Countries decreased from 2.16 to 1.36 $/barrel, while the export price of the same fuel to the Satellites achieved 2.98$/barrel.[43] In 1962, the USSR and the FRG initiated a collaborative production process, importing cast iron for pipe manufacturing from the Soviet Union and compensating West German industrialists for processing and producing welded pipes.[44] Moreover, Germany emerged as a conduit for the supply of Soviet energy to Western Europe, due to its strategic position at the heart of Europe.[45]

In a somewhat ironic twist, the United States government agreed to German-Soviet trade based on pipes and energy fuels, just because – following Rudolph's analysis – Washington thought that Germany was not being able to provide Soviet demand with its pipes for an extended period. However, it became evident that the USA had underestimated the capabilities of the German steel industry.[46]

For years, however, NATO had been monitoring the impact of this cooperation on the development of the USSR. The USA identified a Soviet strategy in that field of trade. In its seven-year plan for 1959-1965, the USSR aimed to increase oil production substantially. Moscow was acquiring a significant quantity of

---

42 Free On Board: term of sale under which the price invoiced or quoted by a seller includes all charges up to placing the goods on board a ship at the port of departure specified by the buyer - <http://www.businessdictionary.com/definition/free-on-board-FOB.html>.

43 *Impact of Oil Exports from the Soviet Bloc*, pp. 110–11.

44 Daniel Kosthorst, 'Primat Der Politik Als Primat Der Bündnispolitik: Zum Streit Um Das Röhrenembargo Gegen Die UdSSR', in *Studien Zur Auswärtigen Politik Der Bundesrepublik Deutschland 1963*, ed. by Rainer Blasius (Berlin, Boston: Oldenbourg Wissenschaftsverlag, 1994), pp. 97–117 (p. 99) <https://doi.org/doi:10.1524/9783486703092-004>.

45 Carter, p. 36.

46 Rudolph, pp. 156–58.

pipes, which could be employed in the future to accelerate its petroleum production programme. Concurrently, American oil companies perceived a threat from the emergence of Soviet competition in the Old World. The USA was afraid that European dependence on the USSR, both economically and politically, could result in the detachment of Europe from NATO. Above all, the US feared an improvement in the USSR's military situation.[47]

The United States government and the directors of oil companies, such as Esso, were engaged in coordinating embargo measures against Russia's energy initiatives, which would have a significant impact on Russia's energy sectors. The USA were aware that European countries would not have agreed with such a pipes embargo promoted directly by the United States, so they were advocating for a NATO initiative.[48] In this way, the USA highlighted its primary role in the establishment of East-West relations, its power in the Atlantic Alliance and in Europe, and its tendency to politicise economic questions. In 1961, NATO actually had begun to consider the critical impact of a major pipe embargo on the construction of the *Druzhba* (Friendship) pipeline from Siberia to Schwedt an der Oder in the GDR. The new pipeline would bring more oil from Siberia to East Germany, which would be refined in Schwedt and reexported to West Germany. The USA soon realised that, while such a measure might have not stopped the project, it could have slowed it down.[49] In November 1962, the North Atlantic Treaty Organization finally agreed to prohibit the delivery of large-diameter pipes to the

---

47 Markus Engels and Petra Schwartz, 'Alliierte Restriktionen Für Die Außenwirtschaftspolitik Der Bundesrepublik Deutschland. Das Röhrenembargo von 1962/63 Und Das Erdgas-Röhren-Geschäft von 1982', in *"...die volle Macht eines souveränen Staates...". Die Alliierten Vorbehaltsrechte als Rahmenbedingung westdeutscher Außenpolitik 1949-1990*, by Helga Haftendorn and Henning Riecke (Baden-Baden: Berlin-Brandenburgische Akademie der Wissenschaften,1996), p. 229 <https://edoc.bbaw.de/frontdoor/index/index/year/2007/docId/362>, p. 229 <http://slubdd.de/katalog?TN_libero_mab2>; Wörmann, xxxviii, p. 29.

48 Rudolph, 163–64.

49 PA AA, B 150 AAPD/5, Aufzeichnung: Großrohrembargo. Handschriftliche Weisung des Herrn Staatssekretär auf anliegender UPI/Reutermeldung vom 26.3.1963, geheim, 2 April1963, fol. 21.

USSR in order to inhibit further German-Russian pipes trade and retroactively the last contract signed in the autumn of the same year between German companies Mannesmann AG, Hoesch and Phoenix-Rheinrohr and the Soviet Union. The US saw the deal as direct support for the leading power of the opposing bloc in an area of strategic military importance.[50]

Given the considerable oil and gas reserves held by Russia and the growing need for foreign fuels in Europe, it was to be expected that both the Soviet Union and the European Community would adopt a more proactive approach to energy policy. However, Adenauer accepted the so-called *"Röhrenembargo"* in exchange for protection and assistance in the event of another attack on West Berlin, despite the potential negative impact on German-Soviet trade and German economy.[51] Once again, the leader of the CDU acted on political impetus, thereby demonstrating his dependence on Western powers in dealings with the USSR and threatening economic stability. Moreover, in 1963, in a moment of parliamentary contention aimed at undermining the legal basis of the embargo, which was also supported by the industrialists, his party succeeded in nullifying the parliamentary votes, refusing to take a decision until it became impossible to withdraw from the NATO amendment, and leaving the decision to impose the embargo in place.[52]

German balance of payments with the Soviet Bloc deteriorated significantly, with the surplus of 1960/61 giving way to a deficit that persisted until 1969. The lack of export trade was particularly pronounced in the heavy industrial sector. To illustrate this point, we may consider the case of Mannesmann AG. In a single year, the company incurred a loss of $25 million.[53] Additionally, the deficiencies in eastern trade were not offset by an expansion in trade relations with other countries, such as the

---

50   Engels and Schwartz, pp. 227–28; Kosthorst, pp. 98–99; 105–7.
51   Rudolph, p. 170.
52   Kosthorst, p. 98.
53   Angela Stent, *From Embargo to Ostpolitik. The Political Economy of West German-Soviet Relations, 1955-1980* (Cambridge: Cambridge University Press, 1981), p. 110.

USA. While the political relations with Moscow, as previously anticipated, underwent a cooling-off period, relations with the Americans were also affected. The relationship between Bonn and Washington was fraught with difficulty at the time, but the German government was reluctant to act against the USA in order to prevent a political crisis.[54] The instability of trade relations, whereby German industrialists would honour the contracts entered into, while the government would block them, gave rise to the suspicion that the Soviet Union would take political measures against the FRG by accusing it of direct contravention of the supply agreements, not respecting international law,[55] and also the agreements and requirements of West German industrialists.[56] This actually represented, following Smirnov, a hostile act against the USSR. This is particularly the case if the act is perceived as a political rather than an economic one. Furthermore, the fact that the decision lacked an economic component, as Secretary Rolf Otto Lahr observed, served to reinforce the conviction of the Soviet Union in that idea.[57]

Fortunately, a mere year after it, the embargo was perceived as a failure. The political objective of vanquishing the USSR in the European market and reducing its influence on the West, as pursued by the USA, had not been achieved. From the outset, European allies such as Italy, Sweden and the UK demonstrated a clear willingness to facilitate trade with the USSR. The overt willingness of a British company to accept a contract with Poland and to work on one with the USSR in February 1963 significantly undermined the credibility and position of the US and the West German government on the embargo.[58] The sanctions were deemed insignificant for the Soviet economy, as

---

54　Wörmann, xxxviii, p. 33.

55　Jüngerkes, p. 191.

56　PA AA, B 2-B STS/152, Aufzeichnung über ein Gespräch zwischen dem Staatssekretär im Auswärtigen Amt Lahr und dem sowjetischen Botschafter Smirnow anlässlich der Überreichung der deutschen Antwortnote zum Röhrenembargo am 11. April 1963 um 12 Uhr im Büro des Herrn Staatssekretärs, fol. 3.

57　*Ibid.*

58　Kosthorst, pp. 110–13.

Russia was gradually modernising its industrial apparatus and the project for the construction of a pipeline was only postponed. Moscow compensated for the lack of German industrial products by importing from other Western countries or Japan.[59] The search for new drilling sites in the area was also under way. Between 1960 and 1970, the USSR demonstrated a significant increase in its annual volumes of gas extraction, with an annual leverage of approximately 16%. In 1965 and 1966, two gas fields were discovered in Russia: the Zapolyarnoye field and the Urengoy field. The Zapolyarnoye field became Russia's number-one gas-producing field, while the Urengoy field was the largest field discovered at the time. This resulted in a notable expansion from 45.3 billion m³ (bcm) in 1960 to 157.4 bcm in 1967 and 197.9 bcm in 1970, positioning the USSR as the second largest global gas producer, trailing only the USA.[60]

Although West-German government was determined to maintain the embargo, in January 1963, under pressure from industrialists, it began to call for certain changes and revisions to the manoeuvre, which could, among other things, exempt contracts signed after November 1962 from the trade embargo or restrict the pool of embargoed goods. Despite the fact that other countries were moving in order not to respect the embargo, it is interesting to note that the Americans rejected the West-German demands and even threatened the Federal Government with charges of breaking the embargo if they officially called for changes.[61] In March, after further discussion, the German government acknowledges the negative feedback in the negotiations with NATO on the changes and emphasises that while it shares the industry's concerns, the pipe embargo is a political rather than an economic issue and that foreign policy aspects must take precedence over economic

---

59   Jüngerkes, p. 200.
60   BArch-Koblenz, B 102/163897, Report of Deutsches Institut für Wirtschaftsforshung, "Bedeutung und Möglichkeiten des Ost-West-Handels mit Energieröhstoffen", March 1973.
61   PA AA, B 150 AAPD/5, Aufzeichnung: Großrohrembargo. Handschriftliche Weisung des Herrn Staatssekretär auf anliegender UPI/Reutermeldung vom 26.3.1963, GEHEIM, 2 April 1963, fols. 25-27.

issues.[62] It is evident that this resulted in an irremediable rupture in the government, until the President of the Parliament declared that the *Bundestag* itself was no longer able to make decisions, as it was not an expression of the majority and the needs of the country.[63] Consequently, in May 1963, West German pipe industries started negotiations with the Soviets again.[64]

The West German government's unfortunate handling of the negotiations between industrialists and NATO ultimately led to Adenauer's resignation in 1963, and Ludwig Erhard became the new Chancellor. With his Minister for Economics Kurt Schmücker and his Foreign Minister Gerhard Schröder he concentrated German political strength in a more flexible Ostpolitik, the so-called 'policy of movement'. This policy, in contrast with Adenauer's 'policy of strength', focused on the Eastern European countries' markets and was based on cooperation in several economic and political fields.[65] The new members of the federal government were aware of the importance of the Soviet Bloc for the German economy. However, they were constrained by the Hallstein Doctrine and the CDU principles, which prevented them from achieving their specific goals and from changing the basic policy towards Moscow. The situation underwent a further transformation at the end of 1966, when Willy Brandt, an exponent of the Social Democratic Party of Germany (SPD), assumed the role of Minister for Foreign Affairs and Kurt Georg Kiesinger, an exponent of the CDU/CSU, became Federal Prime Minister, forming a new government: the "Grand Coalition". Upon the SPD's electoral victory becoming apparent, Moscow demonstrated a willingness to engage with the FRG in a constructive and cooperative manner.[66]

The embargo was officially lifted in November 1966, following a request to NATO signed by several countries, among others the

---

62   *Ibid.*, fols. 39-41.

63   *Ibid.*

64   PA AA, B 2-B STS/152, Telegram sent by Ernst Osterheld to the Ministry of Foreign Affairs, fol. 11.

65   Von Dannenberg, p. 25; Stent, p. 128.

66   Rudolph, pp. 213, 216, 219.

FRG, France, and Italy. Thanks also to the more opened foreign policy of the new government, West German-Soviet trade too had been steadily improving since 1967. Despite the imposition of trade restrictions, which resulted in a negative balance of payments from 1965 to 1968, according to the German Foreign Ministry, imports from Russia had increased by 195% and exports by 314% between 1959 and 1969.[67] Between 1967 and 1968 specifically imports from the Federal Republic of Germany increased by +19%, and then by +37% and +44% in the following two years. Exports to West Germany, on the other hand, grew less strongly, with an average annual growth rate of 6% between 1966 and 1969.[68] Consequently, at the end of the Sixties, the Soviet Union held approximately 1.4% of the total West-German foreign trade. The majority of imports in the FRG consisted of oil and raw materials, while Moscow imported a greater quantity of construction products and chemicals,[69] but also special machinery and steel pipes. (See Table 1)

As it has been shown above Germany regained its position as Moscow's most important Western partner and the USSR remained German biggest socialist trading partner.[70]

For years, industries had been opposed to the government's apparent lack of interest in *Osthandel*. Both Adenauer and Erhard had failed politically and economically with the USSR. During the 1960s, businessmen demonstrated once again that they were the real representatives of German economy. They attempted to facilitate access to credit for the East through engagement with SPD representatives, to invest in the Soviet Bloc and to collaborate with eastern countries on the construction of new petrochemical infrastructure.

---

67 PA AA, B 41 REF IIA 4/84, Aufzeichnung. Stand der deutsch-sowjetischen Handelsbeziehungen: Besprechung im Bundeskanzleramt am 5. Juli 1970, fol. 152.

68 *Sowjetunion 1970*, Allgemeine Statistik Des Auslandes / Länderkurzberichte (Stuttgart und Mainz: Statistisches Bundesamt, 1970) <https://www.statistischebibliothek.de/mir/receive/DEHeft_mods_00080421>.

69 PA AA, B 41 REF IIA 4/84, Aufzeichnung. Stand der deutsch-sowjetischen Handelsbeziehungen: Besprechung im Bundeskanzleramt am 5. Juli 1970, fol. 152.

70 Stent, p. 164.

3.
FROM 1969 TO 1989

3.1 *The new Ostpolitik*

Brandt and Kiesinger paved the way for a new social-democratic *Ostpolitik* in the late 1960s, even though there was strong resentment on the Eastern side, also linked to the new dominant policy and Soviet attitude to the other Republics. After the invasion of Czechoslovakia, at the Polish Communist Party Congress on 12 November 1968, the Soviet party chief Leonid Brezhnev enunciated the so-called "Brezhnev Doctrine", which affirmed Moscow's right to intervene in the affairs of Socialist countries in order to strengthen Marxist-Leninist principles.[1] Brezhnev's discourse had a destructive impact on Western perceptions of the Soviet political order and its reliability. Nevertheless, Kiesinger and Brandt sought to re-establish and perpetuate even poor diplomatic relations with Eastern European countries. They were convinced that it was of vital importance to have close relations with other countries based on mutual trust and spirit of cooperation, even, when possible, with Warsaw Pact countries. They attempted to modify the Hallstein Doctrine, which not only had prevented such relations but also failed to achieve its main goal and amplified the FRG-GDR contrast. They advocated for the "birth defect theory", which posited that collaboration with Eastern countries did not necessitate GDR

---

1   Stephen G. Glazer, 'The Brezhnev Doctrine', *The International Lawyer*, 5.1 (1971), 169–79.

recognition. This exception allowed Bonn to maintain relations with all European states except the GDR.[2]

On the other hand, the Soviet Union was interpreting the growing trade and opening between West Germany and the East in a negative light, viewing it as an expression of revanchism towards East Germany and a threat to the integrity of the Soviet Bloc. In fact, the Grand Coalition did not entirely abandon the Hallstein Doctrine; rather, it modified it. Consequently, despite the German government's decision to diverge from the US in terms of foreign trade policy, Moscow remained sceptical and expanded its trade relations with other European countries.[3]

As evidenced by a 1968 Soviet memorandum, the West German opening was regarded as a manifestation of the latter:

> "The Soviet Union's definite position towards the "Neue Ostpolitik" is designed both to its immediate unmasking and rejection as well as to strengthening the socialist states' united front, according to our jointly taken resolutions. Based on the assumption that imperialism "is pursuing ever more intense efforts directed at political and ideological undermining of the socialist states, against the communist and general democratic movement", the Soviet Union is also intensifying the theoretical confrontation against Ostpolitik as one part of imperialism's ideological diversion This is also served by the further unmasking of the SPD leaders' role in the Grand Coalition."[4]

In 1969 the situation changed. At the beginning of the year there were discussions between the political planners of the major European states and the United States about relations beyond the Iron Curtain, and Egon Bahr, one of the key SPD leaders and political theorists of Brandt's Ostpolitik, stressed the need to ease relations with Moscow with projects that were not perceived as a threat by the Soviets and thus did not challenge

---

2   Rudolf Zundel, 'Das Ende Der Doktrin?', *Die Zeit*, 6 June 1969, 23–24 edition, pp. 7–8.
3   Stent, pp. 137–40.
4   PA AA, MfAA, C 326/77, "Current Essetial Questions in the Soviet Union's Politicals of Ensuring European Security (26 April 1968)", History and Public Policy Program Digital Archive – available online at <https://digitalarchive.wilsoncenter.org/document/110078>.

the sovereignty of the USSR.[5] As in the past, and even more so in the Seventies, Bahr was an advocate of an intensive foreign policy towards the East, and in particular towards the GDR. He was also the author of the phrase *Wandel durch Annäherung*, "change through rapprochement", which he first used in a speech in Tutzing in 1963 to describe the Federal Republic's approach to the GDR.[6] Even then Bahr affirmed that

> "The conditions for reunification can only be created with the Soviet Union. They cannot be achieved in East Berlin, not against the Soviet Union, not without it."[7]

Bahr challenged the US peace strategy for Germany and, by extension, that of Adenauer. He claimed, in some way referencing Armarck's beliefs, that the much-desired German reunification could only be achieved after a series of agreements, transformations, and a long process of cooperation between Germany itself and its counterparts: the USSR and the GDR. Moreover, he proposed that an increase in trade relations would be mutually beneficial to both the FRG and the GDR, subject to certain conditions: it would help material improvement in East Germany and foster a more relaxed atmosphere, thereby facilitating and strengthening the construction of relations between the two parts. Actually, the FRG had already a lower tax burden on trade with East Berlin than other countries, such as France.[8] This was the reason why trade with the GDR was more advantageous and constituted a preferential channel for importing

---

5   Stephan Kieninger, 'Between Power Politics and Morality', in *The Long Détente: Changing Concepts of Security and Cooperation in Europe, 1950s–1980s*, ed. by Oliver Bange and Poul Villaume (Central European University Press, 2017), pp. 281–314 (p. 282) <https://doi.org/10.1515/9789633861295-014>.

6   Jüngerkes, p. 212.

7   Egon Bahr, 'Wandel Durch Annährung. Ein Diskussionsbeitrag in Tutzing. (Redemanuskript)', 1963, Archiv der sozialen Demokratie der Friedrich-Ebert-Stiftung, Bonn <https://www.1000dokumente.de/index.html?c=dokument_de&dokument=0091_bah&object=facsimile&pimage=1&v=100&nav=&l=de>.

8   BArch Berlin-Lichterfelde, DL 2/6271a, Gründe und Ziele der westdeutschen Mehrwertsteuer-Gesetzgebung und ihre Auswirkungen für die DDR im

products from the Bloc, including energy sources. In general, a condition of cooperation with both the USSR and East Germany was, then, more than desirable for economic advantages and a more direct and convenient access to the Eastern Bloc market.

Brandt was convinced of the efficacy of these ideas, and thus began informal discussions with the Soviet government apparatus prior to his election to the Chancellery, with the aim of presenting his policy of détente. These discussions, which were held between the then-Defence Minister Helmut Schmidt and Gromyko, presupposed a normalisation of relations between the FRG and the USSR.[9] These resulted in an informal understanding. Brandt's election as Chancellor, his *Ostpolitik* and the support of German industry reduced both internal and Soviet opposition. Brezhnev moderated his policies with the expectation of a more flexible collaboration and supported the SPD-FDP coalition to come to power, advocating what is known as *"Westpolitik"*.[10]

The more relaxed climate on European soil was joined by one from overseas. At a meeting of the members of NATO's Nuclear Planning Group, Richard Nixon, the new US president, gave a speech on the international framework in which he stressed, among other things, the importance of seeking cooperation with the Soviet Union in order to achieve détente in the field of strategic armaments. This stance dovetailed perfectly with Brandt's intentions.[11] All this ushered in a new era in East-West relations. Indeed, the FRG and the GDR too claimed the historical necessity for a peaceful coexistence of the two German states, the necessity to elaborate an economic and diplomatic agreement which could benefit both, although their antagonistic social systems. Briefly, both state leadership wanted to "achieve a peaceful and secure future [...] the establishment of good

---

Handel zwischen beiden deutschen Staaten, Deckbatt zur Vorlage für die Dienstbesprechung beim Minister für Außenwirtschaft, 19 February 1968.

9   Schmidt, p. 21.

10   For further information, please refer to the following sources: Federica Caciagli, *La Germania Est tra Mosca e Bonn. Ostpolitik e Westpolitik nel Rilancio del Processo di Sicurezza in Europa.1969-1975* (Roma: Carocci, 2010); Lippert, 'The Economics of "Ostpolitik"'; Stent.

11   Schmidt, p. 143.

neighbourly relations between the GDR and the FRG on the basis of equality and the exclusion of any discrimination."[12] From Ulbricht's perspective, the precondition for the conclusion of such an agreement was the FRG's recognition of the German Democratic Republic. This was necessary to ensure the pact's effectiveness and compliance with international law. Brandt's government and subsequent administrations pursued this objective. In fact, Brandt recognised that the FRG's refusal to acknowledge the GDR had diminished its international influence and was now prepared to accept both Polish and Soviet borders and even the GDR as a state in order to facilitate the future reunification of the two Germanies.[13] Actually, the prospect of reunification was one of the factors that led to the conclusion of several agreements between the FRG and other eastern countries in the 1970s.

Concurrently, Brezhnev altered his stance towards the West. Following a protracted period of distrust, Moscow opted to embrace Bonn in order to capitalise on the nascent German government. The Kremlin also had its own political considerations: in the wake of the crisis in Eastern Europe, the USSR sought to reinforce the legitimacy of its influence in its European territories. Additionally, it aspired to deter Germany from aligning with the United States and, conversely, to cultivate a more cordial relationship with Washington.[14]

Brandt's political beliefs and Brezhnev's *Westpolitik* played a pivotal role in the signing of the Moscow Treaty in 1970 between the Federal Chancellor Willy Brandt, his Minister for Foreign Affairs Walter Sheel, and the Soviet Prime Minister Alexei

---

12   'News Conference Remarks by Chairman Ulbricht on Negotiation of a Treaty Establishing Equal Relations Between East and West Germany, January 19, 1970', in *United States-Department of State. Documents on Germany 1944-1985*, Department of State Publication, 9446 (Washington: Department of State, 1970), pp. 1065–67 <https://www.cvce.eu/obj/press_conference_by_walter_ulbricht_19_january_1970-en-413e904a-5a45-4a6b-97d4-cc259bd87efe.html>.

13   Von Dannenberg, p. 31; Stent, p. 155.

14   Stent, pp. 156–57.

Kosygin.[15] This agreement was negotiated by Egon Bahr himself as Special Ambassador in Moscow. The two parties

> "Convinced that peaceful cooperation among States on the basis of the purposes and principles of the Charter of the United Nations complies with the ardent desire of nations and the general interests of international peace; Appreciating the fact that the agreed measures previously implemented by them, in particular the conclusion of the Agreement of 13 September 1955 on the Establishment of Diplomatic Relations, have created favourable conditions for new important steps destined to develop further and to strengthen their mutual relations; Desiring to lend expression, in the form of a treaty, to their determination to improve and extend cooperation between them, including economic relations as well as scientific, technological and cultural contacts, in the interest of both States."[16]

The parties agreed to develop peaceful relations with and among European states, to refrain from the use of force in settling disputes, and to maintain and regard the frontiers, including the Oden Neisse Line, which was the western frontier of the People's Republic of Poland and the frontier between the Federal Republic of Germany and the German Democratic Republic.

From the Soviet point of view, that agreement secured and consolidated Soviet control over Eastern European countries. Conversely, Germany was obliged to clarify its foreign political objectives. Therefore, Sheel incorporated a brief on the Unity of Germany into the treaty, wherein he asserted that such an agreement was not incompatible with the federal political intention of reunifying Germany,[17] as Bahr himself had previously asserted in his commentary on the treaty.[18]

---

15   Von Dannenberg, pp. 46–50.

16   'The Moscow Treaty (12 Aug. 1970)', in *United States-Department of State. Documents on Germany 1944-1985* (Washington: Department of State Publication), pp. 1103–5 <https://www.cvce.eu/obj/the_moscow_treaty_12_august_1970-en-d5341cb5-1a49-4603-aec9-0d2304c25080.html>.

17   Walter Scheel to Andrej Gromyko, 'Brief zur deutschen Einheit', 12 August 1970, pp. 156–57 <https://www.chronik-der-mauer.de/material/180318/brief-zur-deutschen-einheit-12-august-1970>.

18   Willy Brandt, *My Life in Politic* (London: Hamish Hamilton Ltd, 1992) <http://www.cvce.eu/obj/willy_brandt_my_life_in_politics-en-a21dae1a-a392-44c3-9cfd-2017525d1c32.html>.

Even though it can be demonstrated that the principal goals of the Treaty were political, there were, however, also economic interests at stake. Brandt sought a statement from the Russians from the outset that further reparation payments, in addition to those imposed after the war, would not be expected of the FRG. Brezhnev and Kosygin, on the other hand, proposed a cooperation in the economic, scientific and technological spheres, as well as in the exploitation of mineral wealth in Siberia.[19] This was a consistent and persistent issue in German-Russian discussions.

Another challenge the SPD Government had to address at the beginning of the Seventies was the role of Berlin. In fact, the Berlin question constituted a pivotal issue that had to be addressed not merely to resolve political differences, but also economic disputes, as already pointed out. In the context of relations with the USSR, the non-involvement of West Berlin in the agreements between Bonn and Moscow meant that the trade agreements concluded since the late 1950s could not be implemented.[20] At the time, the parties involved in the dispute were able to reach a general agreement. The Four Powers (the United States, the Soviet Union, Great Britain, and France), which had retained responsibility for the divided Berlin since 1949, reached an arrangement over the city's status with the aim of improving the situation of the city, in particular of isolated West-Berlin. The Quadripartite Agreement, which had been in place since March 1970, was closed. Over a 25-year period, West Berlin served as a "front-line city" between the Western and Eastern Bloc. The pact was regarded as the most challenging aspect of Ostpolitik and "one of the most important landmarks on the path of consolidating a lasting peace in Europe and of strengthening security on our continent". Soviet officials asserted that West Berlin was not to be considered a territory belonging

---

19   Brandt.
20   PA AA, B 41 REF IIA 4/84, Aufzeichnung. Stand der deutsch-sowjetischen Handelsbeziehungen: Besprechung im Bundeskanzleramt am 5. Juli 1970, fol. 150.

to the FRG.[21] However, according to Annex IV of the agreement itself, they recognised the existing ties of West Berlin with West Germany and accepted the decision of the Three Western Powers to allow the FRG to represent the interests of the Western Sectors of Berlin in international organisations and international conferences were also acknowledged, as well as the fact that "procedures, international agreements and arrangements entered into by the Federal Republic of Germany may be extended to the Western Sectors of Berlin provided that the extension of such agreements and arrangements is specified in each case". Another significant aspect of the agreement was the Soviet concession of traffic and travel to and from West Berlin. Furthermore, the governments of West Berlin and the GDR were tasked with negotiating an accord that would regulate the transit between the two territories. This treaty also granted the right of West Berliners to visit East Berlin and the German Democratic Republic, and vice versa, for citizens of the GDR and the FRG.[22]

The Four-Powers Agreement also led to the ratification of the Bilateral Basic Agreement or *Grundlagenvertrag*, negotiated by Federal German State Secretary Egon Bahr and State Secretary for West Berlin Affairs Michael Kohl with Honecker's government.[23] The Basic Agreement, signed in December 1972, established the mutual territorial integrity of the FRG and the GRD, as well as their mutual borders, independence, and sovereignty. This marked the inaugural instance of collaboration between the FRG and the GDR following the establishment of both entities. As a consequence of the aforementioned treaty, the

21   'Soviet Commentary on the Quadripartite Agreement', in *United States-Department of State. Documents on Germany 1944-1985* (Washington: Department of State Publication, 1971), pp. 1153–54 <https://www.cvce.eu/obj/soviet_commentary_on_the_quadripartite_agreement_4_september_1971-en-9ffbda8b-c2a1-4aa2-a7a1-5ceec8302be4.html>.

22   'The Quadripartite Agreement on Berlin (3 Sept. 1971)', in *Documents on Germany 1944-1985*, Department of State Publication 9446 (Washington: Department of State), pp. 1135–43 <https://www.cvce.eu/obj/quadripartite_agreement_on_berlin_berlin_3_september_1971-en-9bfcb5f5-8e0d-46ee-9f7f-8e9a7c945fa7.html>.

23   Hermann Weber, *Geschichte Der DDR* (München: Deutscher Taschenbuch Verlag, 1999), p. 291.

FRG and the GDR were admitted to the United Nations in June 1973.[24]

Once the political issues had been officially resolved, in April 1972, Bonn and Moscow were engaged in negotiations for the first trade agreement to go beyond simple trade relation into the area of economic, technical and industrial cooperation, which assumed an intensification of trade relations between the two contracting parties, the long-term "Agreement on Trade and Economic Cooperation".[25] A hybrid German-Soviet Commission for Economic, Scientific and Technological Cooperation was established. The representatives of the German and Soviet governments and economic interests appointed to this Commission were tasked with managing their trade and economic relations. A prominent figure on the commission was the chairman Otto Wolff von Amerongen, who served to illustrate that, despite the growing involvement of the political elite, business and industry representatives continued to play a pivotal role in the German economy. This committee constituted a significant diplomatic instrument for maintaining a degree of autonomy from the European Community, which at the time was exerting control over the foreign policy of its member states.[26]

At the second conference of the Commission, the directive highlighted that the agreement of 12 August 1970 had a positive effect on the economic relations between the two parties. In particular, the delivery of goods from the Federal Republic of Germany to the Soviet Union had increased considerably. In the industrial, economic, scientific and technical fields, the West-East collaboration not only increased but also had the potential to become even more fruitful in the future. This could be achieved through closer cooperation between Soviet organisations and German small and medium-sized enterprises (SMEs). These misperceptions included the price of natural gas, which was perceived as low and favourable in relation to Russian supply

---

24   Weber, p. 293.
25   *"Western Europe: Economic Links with the Soviet Bloc". An Intelligence Assessment*, p. 14.
26   Jüngerkes, pp. 238–39.

and too high from the German perspective in comparison to Dutch deliveries.[27]

Between 1970 and 1973, Brandt also institutionalised relations with other eastern countries through the so-called *Ostverträge*. *With* Poland and Czechoslovakia were closed the Warsaw Treaty and the Prague Treaty. These pacts committed the FRG and its counterparts to respect the inviolability of borders between them and established diplomatic relations to prevent the peace in Europe. These agreements were also entirely consistent with the FRG's security concerns, rather than political considerations. If the economic interest, as asserted by Department III of the West German Foreign Office, was indeed more pronounced for the eastern countries, for the GDR these bilateral agreements were of paramount importance from the standpoint of market security and the development of relations in general. This also contravened the prevailing trend within the EEC of preferring Community agreements to bilateral ones.[28] Between 1971 and 1974 the trade balance with the countries of the Eastern bloc rose from + DM 930 million to + DM 6728 million.[29] (See Table 2)

3.1.1 *First natural gas pipeline deals*

A significant aspect of the trade between Moscow and Western European countries, including Bonn, in the 1960s involved the exchange of primary sources, particularly oil, machinery and large pipes becoming increasingly important following the lift of the *Röhrenembargo*. It is firstly necessary to acknowledge that the changes occurred during this period were also influenced by a shift in ideology and the management of the economic sector.

---

27   BArch-Koblenz, B 102/163897, Protokoll der 2. Tagung der Kommission der Bundesrepublik Deutschland und der Union der Sozialistischen Sowjetrepubliken für wirtschaftliche und wissenschaftlich-technische Zusammenarbeit, 14 Februarz 1973, fol. 76.

28   PA AA, B 41 REF IIA4/84, Aufzeichung. Beziehungen zu den osteuropäischen Staaten. Eventueller Abschluß langfristiger wirtschaftlicher Rahmenabkommen, 2 July 1969, fols. 66-67.

29   'Statistisches Jahrbuch für die Bundesrepublik Deutschland', 1975 (1976), p. 313 <https://www.digizeitschriften.de/id/514402342_1975|log1>.

The advent of the energy crisis prompted the government to begin discussing more thoroughly the concept of energy security, which concerns the use of energy fuels as a form of leverage and has been a topic of debate in the context of war games.[30] The Grand Coalition moved away from the ordoliberal economic approach and instead pursued a strategy of using state levers to create domestic corporate behemoths in the field of energy. The new strategy and the use of firms would help to mitigate the social challenges caused by the introduction of a new hydrocarbon supply chain.[31] The FRG needed a "new order" in energy sector. In 1969, the Federal Minister of Economics and the Federal Minister of Finance, in collaboration with several energy companies, developed the *Basisprogramm für die Mineralölpolitik*, Basic Program for the Mineral Oil Policy, which for the first time explicitly addressed the issue of energy security supply.[32]

In order to comprehend the subsequent events that transpired following this initial encounter between Bahr and their implications for German foreign policy and the economy, it is essential to grasp the fundamental principles of energy security policy.

Energy policy can be divided into three main dimensions:

---

30 The IEA defines energy security as "the uninterrupted availability of energy sources at an affordable price". <https://www.iea.org/about/emergency-response-and-energy-security>. Energy security has two main aspects: reliability of fuels flow and affordability of energy supplies. The first characteristic deals with the uninterrupted possibility to extract and transport fuels directly to the target markets; the second one focuses on the stability of prices. The risks for energy security are associated with the several dimensions of fuels production, transport and selling, with international and national political situations. The main risks related to flows are technical, coupled with the degree of development in the infrastructures used to transport energy fuels. The global dimension of energy markets and the distance between producers and customers increase this aspect; international, it defines a physical unavailability due to political decisions of producers or countries of transit. See Matteo Verda, *Politica estera e sicurezza energetica. L'esperienza europea, il gas naturale e il ruolo della Russia* (Novi Ligure: Epoké, 2012), pp. 30–31.

31 Gross, *Energy and Power*, p. 92.

32 Wörmann, xxxviii, p. 82.

I.   the technical dimension, which concerns the resilience of infrastructures;

II.   the economic dimension, which concerns the opportunity costs of producing or importing energy fuels;

III.   the political dimension, which involves not only internal political issues, but also foreign policy implications, concerning the cooperation between importers and exporters. Moreover, it is essential to preserve the supply stability and diversification and to avoid the use of fuels as political leverage.

It is evident that importers are typically exposed to significant risks, both economically and politically, as a consequence of their reliance on exporters. In the context of energy trade, it is challenging to distinguish between the economic and political dimensions.[33]

As it was previously demonstrated, several key energy policy issues had already been addressed by the time the short coal age had come to an end, when the utilisation of oil was supplanting the one of coal in the context of domestic energy consumption. Regarding crude oil, during the second half of the 1960s, there was an increase in Soviet crude oil exports to the Federal Republic of Germany, and yet by the end of the decade, a shift in oil flows to the United States, which had the effect of disadvantaging other countries due to a lack of American oil stocks. Moreover, German government was apprehensive for the potential increasing influence of OPEC (Organization of the Petroleum Exporting Countries).

When Brandt rose to power as Chancellor, German government had to deal with several problems in the energy security asset of the state:

I.   the energy transition era was not solely driven by domestic demand for increased energy consumption. It was also influenced by the international political instability;

II.   the German petroleum market had yet to diversify its supply sources beyond the Middle East, which had reached its saturation levels. The transition period was not yet complete;

---

33   Verda, pp. 41–50.

III.   the FRG was in a disadvantaged position with regard to the development of natural gas as a source of energy, and its complete dependence on the Netherlands entailed theoretical significant risks;

IV.   the transition era in energy consumption resulted in the collapse of national European production fields and the increasing need for foreign suppliers. This necessitated the delivery of fuels from several different countries in order to ensure energy security.

Moreover, in 1969, another significant shift occurred in German energy policy, which had implications for future supply and economic and political decision-making. Western governments were confronted with the challenge of meeting the growing energy demands of industrial production, particularly in the United States, where five of the "Seven Sisters"[34] were, as well as in West Germany and across all industrialized countries.

The primary objective was, in this scenario, to diversify the sources and suppliers. The USSR seemed to be, again, a great option.

The first European country to enter into an agreement with the USSR for the importation of gas was, however, not the FRG, but Austria. The deliveries were transported to Austria via the "Brotherhood" pipeline (Urengoy-Pomary-Uzhgorod) since 1968. The non-membership of Austria to NATO guaranteed the country a certain degree of neutrality and independence from American pressure, which other countries, such as the FRG, did not have. This facilitated Soviet outreach to Austria and, consequently, the intensification of relations between Vienna and Moscow.[35] Nevertheless, German steel companies were yet engaged in such trade, as they supplied Austria with pipes required for the construction of the Brotherhood pipeline. Consequently, they were able to participate in energy trade between Russia and Western Europe, albeit indirectly, following the lift of the *Röhrenembargo*.[36]

---

34   ESSO-Exxon, BP, Royal Dutch Shell, Chevron, Gulf, Texaco, Mobil.
35   Verda, p. 89; Sorokin, pp. 1659–61.
36   Wörmann, xxxviii, p. 80.

In light of the apprehension of the German government regarding this, subsequent development within the European context served to reinforce West Germany's perception of the USSR as a potential secure supplier, reinforcing this perception to a greater extent. Moreover, the price of Soviet natural gas was more favourable than that of Dutch natural gas. Despite the influence of the USA, Bahr, who in 1968/69 was Brandt's right-hand man, proposed a meeting with Russian representatives to discuss the potential for an increase energy trade between Western Germany and Russia. Brandt and Bahr emphasised the importance of a trade agreement to achieve the political aims of the FRG. In order to accomplish this, Brandt needed to gain the cooperation of the Soviet Union, which could be reinforced by political and strategic imbalances between the two countries, and "it was only through trade that Brandt could overcome Soviet antagonism to the Federal Republic and persuade the Soviet leadership to engage in high-level talks".[37]

Theoretically, Germany should have faced significant risks in signing an energy supply contract with Moscow, given that it was the importer and thus placed itself in a position of dependency on the USSR. Conversely, the Soviet planned economy should not have been adversely affected by eventual supply problems, such as the sudden interruption of flows towards Europe.[38]

If one monitors the situation, it becomes evident that this is not entirely accurate. It is well documented that the Soviets required West Germany for their economic and political strategy abroad in Europe. Furthermore, energy exports to the FRG could be a significant driver of Russian GDP growth. Petroleum was, in fact, one of the most important Soviet export commodities. The volume of exports was directly related to the sale or taxation of hydrocarbons. When hydrocarbon revenues increased, export incomes did so as well.[39] This trend demonstrates the strength of the connection between export and commodities, even in

---

37   Lippert, 'The Economics of "Ostpolitik"', pp. 65–66.
38   Verda, p. 89.
39   *Sowjetunion 1970.*

the middle of the last century, and the crucial role of the energy sector in maintaining and increasing Russia's wealth.

In contrast, West Germany had a saturated energy market, and oil import quota was already at a high level. The objective was to achieve energy diversification and supply in the future, rather than to improve oil supplies. The FRG also desired a strong relationship with the USSR for its internal political reasons and ends.

In the longer term, a new favourable energy exchange with the West would provide Russia with foreign currency and facilitate the development of its export and import capabilities, which were currently limited. This would, in turn, boost German exports of pipes and other industrial goods, while also resolving three German energy security issues:

I. The diversification of suppliers. Although natural gas accounted for only 3.1% of total German energy consumption in 1968, the Netherland was the sole supplier of this fuel.[40] Consequently, the country in question agreed to supplement its natural gas supply with pipelines originating from the USSR, in order to circumvent the potential risk of becoming wholly reliant on Dutch gas.[41] Furthermore, the delivery of Soviet gas would be minimal, thereby maintaining the stability of the German natural gas market and preventing the emergence of an undesirable dependence on Russia.

II. The diversification of sources. The supply of Soviet natural gas, which is not a significant political issue and is cheaper than other fuels, would enable Germany to reduce its dependence on crude oil and coal. Furthermore, it could compensate for the lack of energy resulting from the German decision to withdraw from nuclear power.[42]

---

40 'Entwicklung des deutschen Gasmarktes (monatliche Bilanz 1998 – 2017, Einfuhr seit 1960)' (BAFA) <https://www.bafa.de/SharedDocs/Downloads/DE/Energie/egas_entwicklung_1991.html>.
41 Bros, Mitrova, and Westphal, p. 12.
42 Marshall I. Goldman, *Petrostate: Putin, Power, and the New Russia* (New York: Oxford University Press, 2010), p. 137.

III. It can be reasonably concluded that Russian imports would not represent a significant threat to German energy security. Given the relatively modest volume of these imports, it is unlikely that they would result in a significant degree of German dependence on Russian commodities.[43]

In summary, both countries had multiple reasons – political and economic – that were driving them towards closer energy trade exchanges. It was not inevitable that one country would become dominant or dependent on the other.

Graph 5: Total primary energy consumption in West Germany 1950-70 (in %)

Source: 'Struktur des Energieverbrauchs' (AGEB - AG Energiebilanzen e.V., 2010), Zeitreihen bis 1989 <https://ag-energiebilanzen.de/daten-und-fakten/zeitreihen-bis-1989/>.

Aware that Germany had a saturated market with oil, the Soviet Trade Minister, Nicolai Patolichev outlined the proposal of a natural gas pipeline, which he believed would create a unique opportunity for concrete cooperation projects.[44] He proposed

---

43   BArch-Koblenz, B 102/163897, Report of Deutsches Institut für Wirtschaftsforshung, "Bedeutung und Möglichkeiten des Ost-West-Handels mit Energieröhstoffen", Berlin, March 1973.

44   Lippert, 'The Economics of "Ostpolitik"', pp. 68–69.

Bonn to consider the construction of a pipeline that would run directly from East to West Germany and facilitate the exchange of gas.[45] Despite the initial reluctance of several CDU ministers, Brandt initiated negotiations with the USSR in the energy supply field shortly after his election as a Chancellor.

On 1 February 1970, Patolichev, and the Federal Republic of Germany Minister for Economics, Karl Schiller, signed the "First Natural Gas Pipeline" deal. This agreement stipulated that the USSR would supply West Germany with 3 billion cubic metres (bcm) of natural gas per year, as well as delivering 1.2 million tons of German pipes, five feet in diameter, to the Soviet Union for the construction of the energy infrastructure.[46]

One noteworthy aspect of this treaty was the considerable number of companies that were involved in the signing. These companies were also involved in the Austrian-Soviet agreement of 1968, among them Mannesmann-Export GmbH and Thyssen-Stahlunion-Export GmbH. Furthermore, Ruhrgas AG, the largest natural gas transportation and trading company in Germany,[47] and the Soviet foreign trade company Sojuzneftexport were the key stakeholders.[48]

Another crucial aspect of the agreement pertained to the financing of the deal. Generally, the construction of a natural gas system is inherently costly, particularly in its initial phase. Nevertheless, the subsequent maintenance costs are comparatively lower. This structure ensures the signing of long-

---

45   Stent, p. 166.

46   BArch-Koblenz, B 102/257471, Memorandum of Dr. Plesser and Dr. Lumpe regarding German-Soviet agreements, Bonn, 24 September 1973. The quantities in question, expressed in monetary terms, amounted to approximately 175 million Deutsche Marks (DM) of natural gas per year imported into West Germany and approximately 1.5 billion DM of large pipes to be delivered to the Soviet Union in the 1971-72 period. In PA AA, B 41 REF IIA 4/84, fol. 152.

47   Ruhrgas AG, was established already in 1926. Unlike state-owned companies, Ruhrgas was a public limited company with significant international stakeholders, including BP and Shell, as well as other German private gas producers. Ruhrgas was not subject to the influence of political direction, allowing it to pursue market logic. Wörmann, xxxviii, p. 82.

48   Jüngerkes, pp. 216–17.

term deals, typically 20-year agreements, allowing sufficient time to recoup the investment and reap the benefits.[49] At the time, the USSR lacked the necessary financial resources to contribute to the costs of the pipeline. However, the natural gas did not flow to the FRG until the pipes were sold and the pipelines were completed. Subsequently, a solution was devised to guarantee the contract. This appeared to be a barter agreement, particularly in the initial years, given that the USSR had not paid for the pipes for several years: Otto Wolff von Amerongen facilitated an arrangement through which Moscow could make payments at the outset through gas deliveries.[50] A financing was, indeed, necessary. The Deutsche Bank, as the leading member of the 15 German banks that financed the supply of pipes and technical equipment for the Soviet gas industry (totalling approximately DM 1,412 million) to the Bank for Foreign Trade of the USSR, has been identified as a key player in this transaction.[51] It was agreed, at the end, for a long-term credit. The USSR was able to benefit from advantageous loan conditions. The loan was to be repaid over a ten-year period at an interest rate of 6.25%, with the first payment due at the end of 1972.[52] The German bank had applied for coverage for the delivery of 100 American Caterpillar tractors and 240 pipe-laying cranes with a total value of DM 158.5 million. This agreement was reached between Mannesmann-Export-GmbH and Traktore-Export Moscow on 13 May 1970. The necessity for sourcing the goods from the USA was due to the fact that the special equipment was not manufactured in the requisite form in Germany.[53]

---

49   Another advantage of the NG-agreements in contrast to the oil trade deals is the fuel prices: with a long-time agreement the agreed prices remain low for long time.

50   Carter, p. 38.

51   PA AA, B 41 REF IIA 4/84, Aufzeichnung. Bundesbürgerschaft für ungebundenen Finanzkredit. Einbeziehung eines Auftrages über amerikanische Caterpillar-Traktoren und Kräne im Wert von rd. DM 160 in die Deckung, 10 June 1970, fol. 140.

52   BArch-Koblenz, B 102/257471, Memorandum of Dr. Plesser and Dr. Lumpe regarding German-Soviet agreements, Bonn, 24 September 1973.

53   *Ibid.*

Even though the deal did not yield immediate profits, it was anticipated that it would lead to further agreements and consequently future advantages for German steel industries and the wider economy. Indeed, a few days after the agreement was signed, the West German ambassador in Moscow, Egon Emmel, engaged in discussions with the Russians regarding potential collaboration in the fields of economics, science, and technology. These discussions were met with considerable interest, particularly in the context of chemistry and petrochemistry. Conversely, in 1969 alone, West Germany had supplied Russia with 45% more goods than the previous year, and imports were also continuing to grow. At the dawn of the new agreement for natural gas and large pipes, the impulse to implement trade was therefore particularly high.[54]

The Soviets offered gas at competitive prices with a discount on natural gas deliveries, a strategy they had employed in the 1950s with oil. The lower prices and the significant transaction attracted German industrial representatives, but the issue of credit remained.[55]

In few years, the structural shifts in energy consumption made European industries dependent on foreign fuel imports. Bonn was barely able to supply about half of its energy demand.[56] The country's oil production declined to 7.1%, with the Federal Republic of Germany importing 92.9% of petroleum. The percentage of oil expenditure reached 53.11%. Approximately 54.7% of crude oil originated from Africa, while only 31.8% originated from the Middle East. Furthermore, the percentage of petroleum imported from Russia decreased to 3.2%. With regard

---

54   PA AA, B 41 REF IIA 4/84, Stand der deutsch-sowjetischen Wirtschaftsbeziehungen unter besonderer Berücksichtigung der von Botschafter Emmel Anfang Februar 1970 in Moskau geführten Kooperationsgespräche, 11 March 1970, fol. 172.

55   Walter Nagel, 'Gibst Du Röhren - Geb' Ich Gas', *Die Zeit*, 19 December 1969, 51 edition <https://www.zeit.de/1969/51/gibst-du-roehren-geb-ich-gas/seite-2>.

56   BArch-Koblenz, B 102/163897, Report of Deutsches Institut für Wirtschaftsforshung, "Bedeutung und Möglichkeiten des Ost-West-Handels mit Energieröhstoffen", Berlin, March 1973.

to natural gas, since 1970 the sole supplier was the Netherlands. In contrast with other European countries, during the 1960s the Netherlands increased its production of energy by 24%. Over the course of only five years, the proportion of natural gas consumed increased from 1.22% to 5.37%.[57] The initial forays into the German-Soviet natural gas market constituted an early manifestation of the country's efforts to diversify its energy sources.

The 1973 agreement between Soyuznefteexport and the German Ruhrgas AG, which began the delivery of natural gas via the Czechoslovakian pipeline, can be understood as a consequence of an increased attention to both economic and political interests. The economic interests were those of German industries seeking to improve their competitive positions in the global market and to increase profits. These interests were not, however, totally coupled with domestic energy demand, which was previously met by other supply countries.

As previously stated, the political interests at stake were those pertaining to German-Soviet relations. The end of the Sixties and the early Seventies can be seen as a period when the government prioritised the concerns of industry, recognising the potential of trade as a means of improving the general atmosphere for negotiations and encouraging German-Soviet political compromises on political matters. Following, with the conclusion of the natural gas agreement, significant political accords were negotiated by Brandt and his Russian counterparts, including, as already described, the Moscow Treaty and the Quadripartite Agreement. The government of Brandt was characterised by a focus on the interconnections between international trade and international relations.

What the Chancellor claimed in Saarbrücken in May 1970 was happening:

---

57   BArch-Koblenz, B 102/163897, Report of Deutsches Institut für Wirtschaftsforshung, "Bedeutung und Möglichkeiten des Ost-West-Handels mit Energieröhstoffen", March 1973.

"No domestic reforms without economic growth, and on the other hand: no economic growth in the long term without domestic reforms."[58]

Brandt emphasised and proved the significance of *Osthandel* and *Ostpolitik* in fostering peace and non-violence in Europe:

"The Party Congress welcomes the efforts to reach a non-violence agreement with the Soviet Union and to bring about a general improvement in German-Soviet relations, as well as the initiative to normalise German-Polish relations, taking into account the Polish people's right to retain their present borders."[59]

3.2.1 *Increased German-Soviet Cooperation*

The First Gas Pipeline Agreement constituted the most significant business transaction ever signed by the Federal Republic of Germany and the USSR, because it represented the inaugural instance of numerous agreements concluded between Brand and the Soviet Union under the *Osthandel*. The deal fostered a deeper and more enduring bond between the two countries, as well as greater political stability within the blocs.

Two years later, the Second Natural Gas Pipeline Agreement was signed. The same counterparts — Mannesmann AG, Thyssen, and Ruhrgas AG on one side, and Sojuznefteexport with the Soviet Deputy Foreign Trade Minister Aleksandr Ossipov on the other — agreed on the implementation of the quantity of gas delivered, which increased from 3 to 4 bcm. The agreement stipulated that 80 bcm of gas would be delivered annually, with a total value of DM 4.3 billion. Furthermore, the German industries agreed to provide 1.5 million tonnes of large-diameter pipes until 1975, while the consortium of German banks agreed to reduce the tax rate to 6% for eight and a half years.[60]

---

58 Franz Osterroth and Dieter Schuster, 'Stichtag 11./14. Mai 1970', in *Chronik Der Deutschen Sozialdemokratie* (Berlin: Electronic ed., 2001) <https:// library.fes.de/fulltext/bibliothek/chronik/band3/e235g1652.html>.

59 *Ibid.*

60 BArch-Koblenz, B 102/ 257471, Memorandum of Dr. Plesser and Dr. Lumpe regarding German-Soviet agreements, Bonn, 24 September 1973.

The favourable terms were made possible thanks to a new German financial system, which was considered a turning point in the history of *Osthandel* and had a positive effect on the energy business. German industry representatives, other exponents of the FRG, USSR governments, and German banks agreed to change the credit policy in order to guarantee export credits to the USSR and to facilitate the development of commercial relations between the two countries.[61]

In accordance with the first natural gas agreement, one of the many factors that influenced Bonn's decision of signing another agreement was the search for energy supply diversification. According to federal data on natural gas relations between the FRG and the Netherlands, at the end of 1972 and the beginning of 1973, it was estimated that Dutch stocks would have been exhausted soon. Furthermore, negotiations with Dutch producers were not progressing due to differences of view with German acquiring firms Ruhrgas AG and Thyssengas. These misperceptions included the price of natural gas, which was perceived as low and favourable in relation to Russian supply and too high from the German perspective in comparison to Dutch deliveries.[62] As Ulf Lantzke, Special Counsellor for Energy to the OECD (Organization for Economic Co-operation and Development) Secretary-General, has also stated, a further increase in cooperative actions and consequently in energy import from the USSR would be desirable for reasons of energy security and policy. He highlighted that there had been developments in this area, particularly with regard to the potential for a tripartite agreement between Ruhrgas AG, the National Iranian Gas Company and Sojuznefteexport in the speech between the Soviet General Secretary Leonid Brezhnev and Brandt in Bonn in May 1973.[63] This speech was of great

---

61   Carter, pp. 53–54.

62   BArch-Koblenz, B 102/ 257471, Daten zur niederländischen Erdgaswirtschaft, January 1973.

63   BArch-Koblenz, B 102/ 257471, Letter of Dr. Lantzke regarding the meeting with the soviet gas minister Orudzhev and the deputy soviet minister for the building of oil and gas constructions, 28 September 1973

significance, marking the inaugural occasion on which a Soviet leader set foot on West German territory during the Cold War. Brezhnev repeatedly underscored the economic and commercial, as well as the political, importance of this event. The Soviets were forthright in their intention to expand economic largescale and long-term cooperation with the FRG. Their wealth was based on energy export.[64]

In addition to outlining the Tripartite Natural Gas Agreement, during Brezhnev's visit the 10-year agreement on the development of economic, industrial, and technical cooperation too was signed. This pact provided for the exchange of raw materials and oil and gas with energy technology, industrial plants, and know-how from Germany.[65] Always intended to establish a framework for future energy cooperation, the May 1973 meeting also achieved a political goal: it was promised that the Quadripartite Agreement would have been fully applied. Furthermore, a cultural agreement was signed, which specifically mentioned West Germany and West Berlin.[66]

The growing energy collaboration between Bonn and Moscow in a relatively short period of time had made the Russian market an extremely lucrative and indispensable one for West Germany.[67] This should be a primary consideration when examining Bonn's actions during and in the aftermath of the oil crises.

3.1.3 *Across the pond*

During his government, Brandt repeatedly emphasised the necessity of NATO support for his policies, as demonstrated in speeches given in Saarbrücken. There, the assertion that the

---

64   *Ibid.*

65   Stent, pp. 191–92.

66   Foreign trade, Moscow, no. 12 (1974), pp. 54-55; Bulletin, 22 May 1973; mentioned in Stent, p. 192.

67   Werner D. Lippert, 'European Long-Term Investments in Détente', in *The Long Détente: Changing Concepts of Security and Cooperation in Europe, 1950s–1980s*, ed. by Oliver Bange and Poul Villaume (Central European University Press, 2017), pp. 77–94 (p. 83) <https://doi.org/10.1515/9789633861295-006>.

Federal Republic of Germany had not become an ally of the Soviet Union or its system, but rather a partner in a business-like contract, was made in order to reassure the United States regarding Bonn's reliability.[68] In his work, "Men in Power", Schmidt himself notes that all Western-German chancellors and heads of government never questioned the assumption that state security depended on the United States' strategy towards European countries.[69] However, the *Ostpolitik* and *Osthandel* of Brandt's government, subsequent actions of the Schmidt government from 1974 onwards and Helmut Kohl's administration later appear to represent a significant divergence and an increasing intolerance of European policy, particularly the one of West Germany, towards American strategies, mainly in trade policy.

As previously noted, upon assuming the role of Chancellor, the former mayor of Berlin made several compromises to CDU policy, in alignment with the interests of the USA. These included accepting the post-war status quo and recognizing the GDR as a de facto state. Additionally, he granted the USSR greater economic advantage and political attention, with the long-term objective of reunifying Germany. These strategic decisions were based on a fundamental belief espoused by Brandt: "Détente in Europe is not possible without the participation of the two German States. It is especially not possible without the active involvement of the Federal Republic of Germany, except at the cost of destroying our friendly relations with our partners and allies in the West."[70] However, as Stent emphasised in her book "From Embargo to Ostpolitik", the advent of a new US-Soviet dialogue during the Seventies also facilitated Brandt's strategy in some way.[71]

---

68   Stent, p. 184.
69   Schmidt, pp. 125–27.
70   'Address given by Willy Brandt on the Basic Treaty (Bonn, 15 February 1973)', in *Verhandlungen Des Deutschen Bundestages.*, 81, 14 vols (Bonn: Deutscher Bundestag und Bundesrat, 1972), pp. 534–38 <https://www.cvce. eu/en/obj/address_given_by_willy_brandt_on_the_basic_treaty_bonn_15_ february_1973-en-0154bfcf-07a4-4c97-9ef0-967526b35381.html>.
71   Stent, p. 161.

Prior to 1969, the FRG foreign policy depended on the Western countries and particularly on the USA. The United States had a dominant position in the decision making. Often Washington interfered in European foreign policy and trade policies indirectly, for example through the imposition of embargo lists and NATO amendments. In addition, the United States and major American petroleum companies sought to restrict the Soviet Union's access to the global petroleum market. The United States regarded the Soviet Union as a disruptive influence on the European market, accusing it of dumping petroleum prices and altering the global energy market.[72]

Both the global capitalist interdependence and energy demand expanded significantly during the Cold War. It became increasingly challenging to prevent Russia from becoming integrated into the Western sphere of influence. Already in the late 1960s, the Johnson Administration recognized the necessity for a temporary cessation of hostilities and initiated a process of liberalizing export controls on American *Osthandel*. This culminated in a comprehensive re-examination and revision of the US export control system: the Export Administration Act of 1969.[73]

The advent of Richard Nixon to the presidency marked the beginning of a new era of détente between the USA and the USSR. Nixon and his National Security Advisor, Henry Kissinger, were confronted with the challenges posed by the Eastern Bloc, which focused primarily on the military sector and the war in Vietnam. Indeed, one of the initial measures implemented by Nixon was the continuation of Johnson's arms control negotiations. This involved the construction of a limited anti-ballistic missile defense system around Moscow and the initiation of strategic arms limitations talks (SALT).[74] Furthermore, the United States of America, and the Union of Soviet Socialist Republics entered into an agreement in September 1971 with the intention of reducing the risk of nuclear war. This was believed to be in the interests of

---

72   Goldman, p. 45.
73   Wörmann, xxxviii, p. 39.
74   SALT: <https://history.state.gov/milestones/1969-1976/salt>.

strengthening international peace and security.[75] Both Nixon and Kissinger were then primarily concerned with the military sphere and were critical of the proposed opening of trade relations with Russia. This was in contrast with their European counterparts, who were signing agreements with the USSR based on the same aim of preserving security, but concerning social, political and also commercial fields. Instead, the USA sought to use economic questions as political weapons to continue a conflict against their ideological enemy. As Kissinger itself claimed "Expanding trade without a political quid pro quo was a gift; there was little the Soviets could do for us."[76]

Nevertheless, they entered into trade agreements with the Soviet Union, firstly in 1971 concerning the export of American agricultural products and secondly in 1972. As a result of these pacts, trade between the two blocs grew rapidly in the following years. In fact, the total American-Soviet trade turnover was almost four times as large in 1972-74 as it was in 1969-71.[77]

However, Nixon and Kissinger generally underestimated the importance of the Soviet market, both for Washington and for Bonn. They did not believe that *Ostpolitik* would succeed. This may have been the reason why Brandt was given a free rein to prosecute his Eastern policy. Moreover, they did not perceive trade as a matter of greater consequence than economics. They failed to grasp the significance the Soviets attached to trade, and consequently failed to recognise that Soviet-West German

---

75   'Agreement between the United States and the Soviet Union on Measures for Reducing the Risk of Outbreak of Nuclear War (Washington, September 30, 1971)', in *Western European Union Assembly-General Affairs Committee: A Retrospective View of the Political Year in Europe 1971* (Paris: Western European Union Assembly - General Affairs Committee, 1972) <https://www.cvce.eu/en/obj/agreement_between_the_united_states_and_the_soviet_union_on_measures_for_reducing_the_risk_of_outbreak_of_nuclear_war_washington_30_september_1971-en-fd9101b8-15c7-494c-a763-a384c58fa394.html>.

76   Kissinger, *White House Years*, p. 152, mentioned in Lippert, 'The Economics of "Ostpolitik"', p. 73.

77   Daniel Yergin, 'Politics and Soviet-American Trade: The Three Questions', *Foreign Affairs*, 55.3 (1977), 517–38 <https://doi.org/10.2307/20039684>.

pipeline deals would have a negative impact on American influence within European countries.[78]

The US opening period to the East was circumscribed and short, because political-ideological considerations once again assumed greater importance than economic ones. Consequently, the United States was never prepared to risk a political crisis. In point of fact, preliminary discussions between Soviet Deputy Foreign Trade Minister Ossipov and the leaders of American Consortium Tenneco (regarding the North Star Project) and the Occidental Petroleum Company and the El Paso Gas Company (regarding the Yakutsk Project) concerning the development of Siberian natural gas reserves and the construction of LNG processing facilities failed to reach a conclusion in 1974.[79] The reasons for this failure were numerous, including the lack of investment in the project, the introduction of the Jackson-Vanik amendment, which was later incorporated into the Trade Act of 1974, and the American refusal to guarantee the MFN status to Russia in exchange for increased trade. This repoliticized Soviet-American relations and made them worse.[80]

3.2 *Chess Moves in the Oil Crisis Games*

In October 1973, the Yom Kippur War commenced, precipitating a global energy and economic crisis. In response to the decision of the United States and several European countries, including the Netherlands and Portugal, to supply and support Israel against Egypt, OPEC suspended oil exports to those countries. This embargo resulted in a doubling of Middle Eastern oil prices, which initiated the first oil shock.[81] All domestic,

---

78   Lippert, 'The Economics of "Ostpolitik"', p. 81.

79   Wörmann, xxxviii, p. 93.

80   Lippert, 'The Economics of "Ostpolitik"', p. 78.

81   A plethora of information, historical and political analysis on the oil crisis can be readily accessed. This report, for instance, will present a number of findings: *Oil Shock. The 1973 Crisis and Its Economic Legacy*, ed. by Elisabetta Bini, Giuliano Garavini, and Federico Romero (London/New York: I.B. Tauris, 2016); Rüdiger Graf, 'Making Use of the "Oil Weapon": Western

public, and industrial apparatus of every country was susceptible to any disruption in the flow of fuels from that region, since Western industrial countries had become heavily reliant on the Middle East in recent years, particularly on its energy resources, and faced a high risk of energy insecurity.

The different perception of the Yom Kippur war by the USA and the FRG resulted in the healing of a rift between the two powers that had remained for several years. The United States' dependence on Middle Eastern oil imports was minimal, and Washington had no long-term economic ties with Moscow. Consequently, the United States was not significantly affected by the crisis and could openly express its criticism of Soviet intervention in the conflict. This was one of the reasons why Washington and Bonn were unable to formulate a unified response to the war.[82] Other NATO countries in Europe, which were heavily dependent on Middle Eastern supply, sought to disassociate themselves from American leadership in a coalition of importing countries against OPEC. They chose to refuse allowing the US Middle East policy to supply Israel from bases on their territories and asserting their independence in deciding their energy strategy.[83]

Germany, however, found itself in a difficult position. It had to tread carefully to maintain cordial relations with both the Soviets, in order to guarantee gas deliveries and continue the

---

Industrialized Countries and Arab Petropolitics', *Diplomatic History*, 36.1 (2012), 185–208; Ennio Di Nolfo, *Storia delle Relazioni Internazionali II – Gli anni della Guerra Fredda 1946-1990* (Roma-Bari: Laterza, 2008), pp. 608–12; Leonardo Maugeri, *L'era del petrolio: mitologia, storia e futuro della più controversa risorsa del mondo*, trans. by Alessandro Maugeri, *L'era del petrolio : mitologia, storia e futuro della più controversa risorsa del mondo*, Serie bianca (Milano: Feltrinelli, 2006), pp. 125–41; Rainer Karlsch and Raymond G. Stokes, *Faktor Öl. Die Mineralölwirtschaft in Deutschland 1859-1974* (München: C.H. Beck, 2003).

82   Dankwart A. Rustow, *Who won the Yom Kippur and Oil War?* in Demidova, 'The Deal of the Century: The Reagan Administration and the Soviet Pipeline', p. 112.

83   Giuseppe La Barca, 'The Oil Shock, the Partial Recovery and Their Impact on Trade Policies Across the Atlantic', in *The US, the EC and World Trade: From the Kennedy Round to the Start of the Uruguay Round* (London: Bloomsbury Academic, 2016), p. 51.

Ostpolitik projects, and with Washington, which it still depended on for military support. At the outset, Bonn pursued a policy of 'strict neutrality', neither opposing Washington nor Moscow.[84] However, when the federal government became aware that Richard Nixon was supplying Israel from German territory, it publicly denounced American conduct. The ministry statement openly claimed that the FRG 'has firmly decided not to be drawn into the Middle East conflict. It sticks by its neutrality and by the balanced nature of its foreign policy, despite the strain of the new Middle East war. It is convinced that this is the best way to serve the interests of creating a lasting and just peace'.[85] Even at the trade level, the shock had the effect of inhibiting imports from overseas.[86]

In order to mitigate the adverse effects of the crisis on the domestic economy, the *Bundestag* enacted the Energy Security Act on 9 November 1973. It granted the Federal Government the authority to implement temporary measures to rationalize the use of energy. These measures included the regulation of the production, use, transport, delivery, and purchase of crude oil, oil products, machinery, and other energy fuels. Furthermore, the Act stabilized the verification and communication requirements for energy fuels.[87] It became evident that a strategy of diversification of suppliers was necessary in order to offset the consequences of the embargo, secure the energy supply, meet domestic energy demand and reduce state vulnerability to energy fuels in the future. One solution to this problem was to encourage as much energy production as possible from as many different producers as possible. Russia was regarded as one of the most favourable and secure suppliers.[88] In point of fact, the USSR previously declined to participate in OPEC. Then, during the initial years of

---

84   Lippert, 'The Economics of "Ostpolitik"', pp. 79–80.

85   'Bonn Bids U.S. Halt Arms to Israel via Germany', *New York Times*, 1973, 20.

86   Dankwart A. Rustow, 'Who Won the Yom Kippur and Oil Wars?', *Foreign Policy*, 17, 1974, 166–75 (p. 168) <https://doi.org/10.2307/1148119>.

87   BArch-Koblenz, B 122/8526, Situation der Energieversorgung; Maßnahmen zur Sicherung der Versorgung, 23 November 1973.

88   Goldman, pp. 46–47.

the 1970s, it capitalised on the situation, increasing its political influence over OPEC countries and enhancing its image in the eyes of European countries. This enabled the Soviet Union to consolidate its market position in the FRG and also facilitated the expansion of the GDR into West Germany.

The process was not straightforward, and initially, even trade with Russia slowed down. In the two months following the sharp decline in oil supply, the German Minister for Economics Hans Friderichs calculated a rapid general rise in price and a challenge to the work of companies and industries, in addition to an estimated loss of about 15-20% in deliveries of crude oil and oil products by the end of the year. One of the companies most significantly impacted by the crisis was Veba-Chemie AG, a German state-owned energy company. Since 1959, Veba AG had been receiving Russian oil used in its refinery through Bomin GmbH. In 1973, the German-Soviet collaboration in this field underwent a transformation. In accordance with an agreement signed in December 1972, Russia was obliged to deliver 3.4 million tons of crude oil to Veba AG. However, it only fulfilled a portion of this obligation and additionally supplied Arabian oil to the FRG. Consequently, due to the global economic crisis, Veba AG was compelled to modify and increase the price it paid for the commodity, also retroactively. The price for the deliveries in 1974 remained undecided in January of that year, and the German company was unaware of when Russia would supply another stock of oil. This resulted in a further temporary disruption to German petrochemical production.[89]

Although in 1973 there was a negative trend in the average of Soviet oil delivered to the FRG (-3.88%), while federal expenditures exhibited a positive trend (+8.46), an increase in the amount of trade with the USSR and oil-exporting countries in general was observed after 1973. In 1974, the quantity increased by 10.37%, and more interestingly, the oil imports expenditure percentage in relation to 1973 rose to +228% (See Graph 5). In

---

89   BArch-Koblenz, B 102/240644, Letter from Dr. Bennigsen to Dr. Friedrichs, Lieferung von russischem Rohöl, 7 January 1974.

the first 11 months of 1974, West Germany, Europe's largest oil consumer, paid $8.5 Mrd to oil☐producing countries for imports but also sold them $3.6 Mrd of German goods. At the same time Bonn also increased its surplus in trade with Eastern Europe by 70%.[90]

Graph 6: West German Imports of Soviet crude oil and shale oil

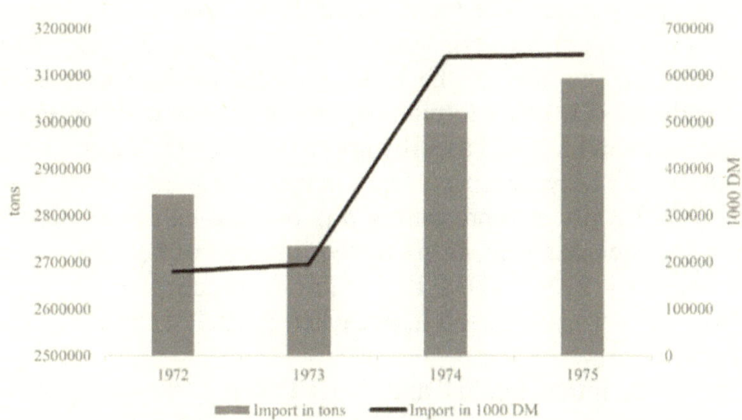

Source: Sowjetunion 1977, Allgemeine Statistik des Auslandes / Länderkurzberichte (Stuttgart und Mainz: Statistisches Bundesamt, 1977), p. 139 <https://www.destatis.de/GPStatistik/content/below/index.xml>.

The rise in import prices resulted in higher prices for equal or even lower quantities of hydrocarbons. The surge in Soviet export prices for petroleum products also led to a minimal decline in total German expenditure on oil, in relative terms. The FRG had to withdraw Soviet petroleum products from bonded storage for domestic consumption, with the objective of narrowing the gap. Concurrently, a portion of the oil that was

---

90   Paul Kemezis, 'West German Trade Surplus Set a Record in 1974', *New York Times,* 30 January 1975 <https://www.nytimes.com/1975/01/30/archives/west-german-trade-surplus-set-a-record-in-1974.html>.

typically reexported was also removed from bonded storage for domestic consumption.[91]

Following the surge in oil market prices in the wake of the shock, East Berlin too intensified its trade across the border in petrochemical products refined within its territory from Soviet oil. The special tariffs in place on products traded between East and West Germany also made it advantageous for Bonn to utilise this supply partner. The GDR promptly leveraged its privileged position in the energy crisis to boost sales of diesel, petroleum, and fuel oil, initially to the FRG, but also to West Berlin. By the end of 1973, East-German exports of refined oil products to these partners had increased by approximately 15.5% compared to the previous year. In currency terms, these exports totalled DM 272.3 million, representing a two-and-a-half-fold increase from the previous year. In particular, the sale of heating oil had increased by 21.9% (DM 19.2 million), crude petrol by 22% (DM 3 million), and gasoil had reached 801,047 t and DM 171.6 million.[92]

In 1974, Intrac GmbH and AHB Chemie, the two leading East German foreign trade companies, sold 1.5 million tonnes of petroleum products with a value of VE 401.2 million to Rex Handelsgesellschaft, an East German company involved in the manufacture of the highest quality industrial products.[93]

---

91   *Reconciliation of Soviet and Western Foreign Trade Statistics* (Washington: Central Intelligence Agency, May 1977), pp. 67–69, General CIA Records <https://www.cia.gov/readingroom/docs/CIA-RDP08S01350R000602080001-1.pdf>.

92   BArch Koblenz, B 206/1613, DDR-Bezüge 1973 deutlich erhöht, 17 May 1974, fol. 38.

93   M. Judt, *KoKo - Mythos und Realität. Das Imperium des Alexander Schalck-Golodkowski…*, cit., p. 66.

Graph 7: Value of petroleum product exports from the GRD to the FRG and West Berlin (In Mio Valutamark)

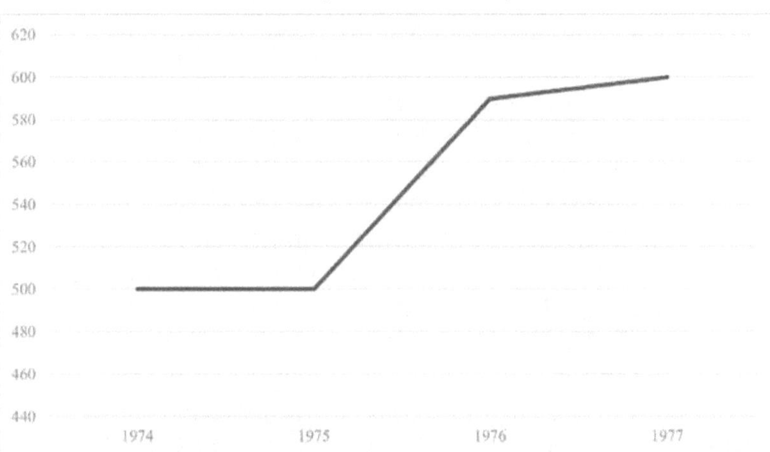

Source: BArch Berlin-Lichterfelde, DL 226/1691, Anlage an der Vorlage für das Politbüro des ZK der SED "Sicherung der Exporte der DDR nach Westberlin in Bezug auf Mineralölerzeugnisse und Baustoffe, 5 January 1978, fol. 365.

The first oil shock coincided with a swap in the supply of West German energy resources. By an ironic turn of events, just five days after the onset of the crisis, Russia began delivering natural gas to West Germany through its first Soviet natural gas pipeline. In 1973, indeed, Mannesmann AG, Thyssen and Ruhrgas AG implemented the first natural gas agreement in accordance with the April Ossipov-Ruhrgas proposal.[94] This event led to an intensification of the Soviet energy trade with West Germany, in addition to the application of German ministry guidelines for addressing the crisis, including the substitution of oil with other energy fuels, such as coal and natural gas, and the diversification of energy suppliers.

---

94   Analyses conducted by the Deutsches Institut für Wirtschaftsforschung indicate that prior to 1973, the Soviet Union had only supplied the Federal Republic of Germany (FRG) only with oil. However, from that year onwards, imports of natural gas commenced.In BArch Koblenz, B 136/6556, Erdöl und Erdgas im Westhandel der Sowjetunion, 22 May 1974, fol. 87.

The policy of consolidating the established relations between the FRG, a country that imports energy, and the USSR, a country that produces energy, perpetrated by German companies and the German government in the months after the Middle Eastern crisis reflected also Otto von Amerongen's ideology. He asserted that in the circumstances, it was imperative not to pursue the European "raw material policy," but rather to implement a "cooperation policy," which would strengthen mutual trade relations with the Soviet Union. He argued that these commercial ties could serve as a stabilizing influence in the German balance of trade.[95]

In a speech of the Chancellor Brandt with the Deputy Chairman of the USSR Council of Minister Ignatij Novikov held in Bonn in January 1974, an increase in the amount of gas delivered from the USSR to the FRG in that year was guaranteed. Moreover, as reported by Novikov in that same speech, based on Commission data, commercial exchanges between the FRG and the USSR in 1973 had increased considerably, by 40%. It was therefore desirable for both sides to enhance cooperation between businesses, as well as to find a solution for planned projects, such as the supply of West Berlin or the question of Iranian gas throughout Soviet territory. In this context, Novikov indicated his willingness to participate in the proposed triangular agreement and to engage in the ongoing negotiations. Fortunately, at the same time, Iran itself agreed to the project, offering approximately 13 billion cubic metres per year. Brandt and Hans Friedrichs, his Minister of Economics, were highly enthusiastic about this opportunity, which was not only of significant economic importance but also of great political significance. Such a project would serve to demonstrate that different countries could collaborate for the mutual benefit of peace and security.[96] The German company Ruhrgas AG was obliged to conclude the tripartite natural gas agreement with

---

95   BArch-Koblenz, B 122/8526, Wortlaut der Rede des Präsidenten des Deutschen Industrie- und Handelstages (DIHT), Otto von Amerongen, vor der Industrie- und Handelskammer Hannover-Hildesheim am 14.1.1974, fols. 208-209.

96   BArch-Koblenz, B 102/163897, Letter from Dr. Fischer to Dr. Geisendörfer, Attachment "Gespräch des Herrn Bundeskanzlers am 18. Januar 1974 mit

Russia and the National Iranian Gas Company. This entailed controlling the negotiation and contract terms, with the objective of finalising the agreement as soon as possible.[97] In the meantime, in response to the growing demand for natural gas in Germany, Soviet Minister Ossipov proposed an additional contract to the first natural gas pipeline agreement, which would increase the volume of gas delivered by 3 billion cubic metres per year.[98]

In April 1974, prior to Brandt's resignation, the Soviet Union proposed another agreement on the same model as the previous ones. The proposed agreement would increase the amount of gas delivered by 2.5 bcm/y, as well as establishing a sale pipe network with an estimated cost of DM 1.2 billion. Additionally, the financial terms would undergo a change, with a rate of 6% over an eight-and-a-half-year period. At the same time, improvements were also made regarding crude oil. As previously indicated, at the end of 1973, there were discrepancies in oil supply between the USSR, Bomin and Veba AG. Consequently, it was resolved that the deficit of 1973 (236,000 t) would be delivered from August 1974 at a price of 3.5 $/barrel. [99]

---

dem Stellvertretenden Vorsitzenden des Ministerrats der UdSSR, Herrn Novikow", 19 January 1974.

97 BArch-Koblenz, B 102/240664, Letter from Dr. Rohwedder to Dr. Sahm, "Ihr Fernschreiben vom 5.3.1974 Nr. 454", 6 March 1974.

98 BArch-Koblenz, B 102/257471, Letter of Dr. Lumpe regarding German-Soviet negotiations about the Natural Gas/Pipes credit, "Besuch des sowjetischen stellvertr. Außenhandelsministers Ossipow bei Herrn Minister Dr. Friedrichs", 22 April 1974.

99 BArch-Koblenz, B 102/163897, Note of Dr. Jahnke regarding German-Soviet trade business, "Gespräche Staatssekretär Dr. Rohwedder – Stellvertretender Außenhandelsminister Ossipow am 22.April 1974", 25 April 1974, fols. 178-180.

Graph 8: Soviet Export to Western Industrial Countries

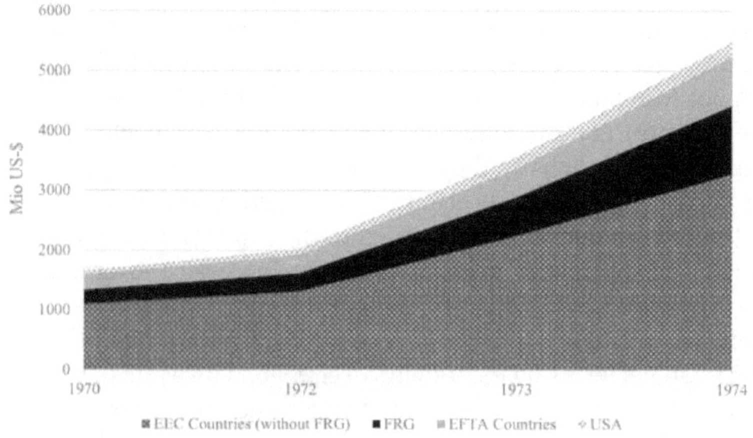

Source: Sowjetunion 1977, p. 129.

From the German perspective, the USSR was becoming one of the most significant energy trade partners. The statistical data concerning Soviet exports to Western industrial countries demonstrated a notable shift in the international trade market in the first half of the 1970s, increasing from $2,766 million in 1970 to $3,411.6 million in 1972. This trend continued, with exports reaching $5,680 million in 1973 and $8,044 million in 1974, representing a notable increase of 136% between 1972 and 1974. For instance, Russia was unable to guarantee a reliable supply of petroleum due to the depletion of its oil reserves, but it could rely on substantial natural gas reserves. Moreover, it was more straightforward and cost-effective for European countries to import this fuel from the USSR than from the USA.[100]

---

100 Demidova, 'The Deal of the Century: The Reagan Administration and the Soviet Pipeline', p. 113.

3.2.1 *From Brand to Schmidt*

With Brezhnev, Brandt had created an equilibrium based on the normalization of relations, which led to the completion of the bilateral phase of Soviet-German détente.

The Chancellor had concentrated not only on trade but also on political and diplomatic rapprochement with Moscow and all Eastern countries. He had overcome the barriers to trade that the CDU had erected and had made the FRG more autonomous from NATO and the USA. In his autobiography "My Life in Politics", Brandt recalled the signing of the Basic Agreement and claimed that:

> "It is certain that no more than we had achieved could have been achieved at the beginning of the Seventies."[101]

Brandt had successfully negotiated several post-war treaties with other countries, which had resolved a number of outstanding issues. These included the question of Germany's geographical location and borders, which were settled by the Moscow, Warsaw and Prague Treaties. The question of Germany's division was temporarily resolved by the Basic Agreement, while the Berlin question was settled by the Four Powers Treaty.[102] Brandt also handled trade issues concerning the distribution of roles between the state and industry. In point of fact, a close collaboration was established between the government and industry based on the division of tasks in trade negotiations. German companies were able to assume an increasingly prominent role in the negotiation of energy agreements with the Soviets, without contravening the directives of the Federal Government. This was evidenced by a number of documents reporting on the content of speeches delivered by Soviet representatives to exponents of Ruhrgas AG, Bomin, Veba AG, Thyssen and other similar entities. In 1974, the President of *Bundesverband der Deutschen Industrie* Friedrich Bohl officially

---

101 Brandt, pp. 216–18.
102 Stent, p. 186.

asserted the significance of separating companies and the state in the decision-making process for an agreement. He argued that companies should be responsible for selecting and coordinating the supply, while the state should oversee the provision of credits, guarantees, and taxes.[103]

Brandt's foreign policy and *Osthandel* had a foundamental impact on Germany's wealth and strength. Undeniably, West Germany had enhanced its foreign policy and international standing in few years. But in mid-1974, Willy Brandt was embroiled in the Guillaume affair and resigned his office in May. The Federal Minister of Foreign Affairs Walter Schiller became acting Chancellor for a while before being elected shortly after as the President of West Germany.

Helmut Schmidt was appointed as Head of government. He rose to power without the support in the governmental team of the two politicians who had first worked for *Osthandel*. However, he brought a depth of expertise on both economic and defence policy to the role, as he had previously served as both Minister of Defence and Minister of Finance under Brandt's government. At the outset of his Chancellorship, his skills were demonstrably crucial. In his inaugural address, Schmidt asserted his intention to build upon Brandt's legacy in fostering East-West rapprochement, because he was aware it was fundamental for German welfare. Schmidt was actually firmly convinced of the value of engaging in dialogue with other leaders, particularly Brezhnev. He demonstrated great resilience in maintaining these conversations, even during periods of heightened stress and adversity. When necessary, Schmidt was willing to utilize unconventional communication channels to ensure the continuity of this dialogue.[104]

---

103 BArch-Koblenz, B 122/8526, Note of Dr. Posdach regarding BDI proposals about resource policy, "Schreiben von BDI-Präsident Bohl an Bundeswirtschaftsminister Friedrichs vom 22.04.1974", 9 May 1974.

104 Stephan Kieninger, 'Diplomacy beyond Deterrence: Helmut Schmidt and the Economic Dimension of Ostpolitik', *Cold War History*, 20.2 (2020), 179–96 (pp. 180–81).

This combination of skills made Schmidt a fundamental figure in West Germany and across the Western world. However, the Chancellor was confronted with an unprecedented economic crisis, which demanded immediate attention.

Since the mid-1960s, the Fordist-Keynesian model has been in a state of decline. The Western world was awash with surplus funds but lacked suitable investment opportunities. This led to a rise in inflation, which was further exacerbated by the dollar crisis and the oil shock. A macroeconomic analysis of the FRG in 1974 revealed an inflation rate of 7%, in comparison to 2% at the beginning of the Brandt Era. The unemployment rate was a cause for serious concern, and economic growth was observed to be below the 7% recorded in 1969, with a decline of over 1% in 1974.[105] The circumstances compelled Schmidt to implement a policy of monetary stringency. Despite the economic crisis, and the restrictive monetary policy adopted by the government, the German trade balance remained robust. As observed by the New York Times, West Germany's trade surplus in 1974 reached a record $22 billion.[106] Following the period of decline, Germany began a recovery in 1976. The Deutschmark subsequently emerged as a strong European currency.[107]

This situation inevitably influenced some of Schmidt moves towards the trade with the USSR too.[108] Firstly, he had reservations about the West German-Soviet Commission for Economic, Scientific and Technological Cooperation. He was concerned about the undue influence and autonomy of German industry representatives on the Commission, including the figure of Otto Wolff von Amerongen. Another point of contention between Brandt and Schmidt was the issue of loans. This reflected their difference in approach to foreign relations with the USSR. Even during his tenure as the country's finance minister,

---

105 Jüngerkes, pp. 40–41.
106 Kemezis.
107 La Barca, p. 111.
108 Kristina Spohr, *The Global Chancellor - Helmut Schmidt and the Reshaping of the International Order* (Oxford: Oxford University Press, 2016), pp. 10–11.

Schmidt demonstrated a reluctance to grant the Soviets undue financial advantages. Upon assuming the role of Chancellor, however he continued to refrain from investing in Eastern Europe in a manner that would have been perceived as overly favourable by the Soviets.[109] Actually, he knew German-Soviet trade contributed to the equilibration of balance of trade during the crisis.

3.2.2 *Mid-decade Multilateral Agreements*

The trade relationship between the USSR and the FRG in the mid '70s did not differ significantly from that described for the first part of the decade. Despite the increase in imports of oil and gas in the 1970s, the amount of Soviet exports and imports grew only slightly in relation to all trade movements of the Federal Republic. The composition of exported goods remained consistent with what was observed in previous decades, with products of heavy industry from the FRG and raw materials and energy fuels from the Eastern countries.[110] From another perspective, Germans believed that the Soviet demand for specific German goods created employment opportunities, for instance in the industry of large pipes, which were the most sought-after commodities. In this context, the implementation of mutual trade could also benefit the German labour market. However, the liberalisation of trade with Eastern countries had a negative impact on German industry as a whole. It had to navigate two key challenges: firstly, the challenge of competing with Western countries in the East, particularly in the American market;[111] and secondly, the challenge of navigating the crisis, which led to a revaluation of the Soviet market and its political security, achieved through intergovernmental agreements.[112]

---

109   Jüngerkes, pp. 245–47.
110   *Ibid.*, p. 244.
111   As it has been referred above, just before the crisis Nixon and Kissinger have begun to stipulate trade agreement with the USSR.
112   Wörmann, xxxviii, pp. 53–55.

Notwithstanding his regard for the growing influence of industrialists, upon assuming power, Schmidt developed a productive working relationship with the *Osthandlers*. Both Bonn and Moscow were eager to continue and implement long-term cooperation. During the first months of his government, Schmidt made significant advancements in foreign trade energy projects and continued to close important frameworks. He devoted particular attention to the trend in natural gas trade. This trend was in line with that observed in all European countries and discussed above: diversification of energy fuel sources, with a preference for a cheaper and faster option, namely natural gas from the Soviet Union.

In addition to the 1972 agreement on cooperation in economic and scientific matters, the addendum to the first natural gas import agreement was still under negotiation when Schmidt assumed the role of Chancellor. The Federal Chancellor and the Federal Minister of Interior Hans Dietrich Genscher in six hands along with Brezhnev closed an agreement about the future collaboration in economic, industrial and technical fields, in which the first five articles concerned energy questions.[113]

Mannesmann AG, Thyssen and Ruhrgas AG worked out in October 1974 the third natural gas agreement, in line with Ossipov-Ruhrgas speech of April. The Soviets agreed to deliver to West Germany about 9.5 bcm of natural gas in exchange of 950,000 tons of large pipes.[114] The closing of the so-called "Third Natural Gas Agreement" gave even more importance to the other agreements, since the deliveries from or throughout the USSR to the FRG would achieve 16 bcm/y, which in projections to the 1985 would represent 18,5% of German natural gas.

These high figures regarding Soviet supply to the FRG were one of the factors prompting Bonn to pursue new energy business with other countries in order to implement diversification strategies,

---

113 "Abkommen über einzelne Fragen des weiteren Ausbau der Zusammenarbeit auf wirtschaftlichem, industriellem und technischem Gebiet", 25 Oct. 1974, cit. in Carter, p. 72.
114 Rudolph, p. 318.

such as those with Iran.[115] In mid-1974, the negotiations between Russia, Iran and West Germany for the Tripartite Agreement, also known as IGAT II, were entering the final phase. Following a telegram from Tehran, it was concluded in the summer that the dispute about prices between Moscow and Tehran had been resolved.[116] In the subsequent stages of the project, other foreign partners were involved, including Gaz de France, SNAM (ENI) and ÖMV – Österreich. The financing plan was also clarified. In a speech between Schmidt and Soviet Prime Minister Kossygin, it was indicated that Germany would be responsible for providing credits to Iran and also to Russia for the pipes. However, Schmidt proposed private financing, with the involvement of foreign credit markets, and the federal government would only be responsible for providing guarantees.[117] Schmidt was particularly interested in the project because the gas transported through the USSR and the GDR to the FRG were projected to reach, basing on the data in January 1975, 18 bcm /y.[118] The establishment of such a financing and forms of credit in Iran and the USSR created a general interest in fulfilling obligations and supplying gas, thereby reducing the risks of sudden withdrawn for both parties. Furthermore, in March 1975, final contractual requirements were established, stipulating that the amount of gas to be delivered was approximately 11 bcm/year. Of this, 5.5 billion was to be delivered to the FRG, with the remaining 5.5 billion to be delivered to France, Italy and Austria. The delivery was scheduled to commence in 1980 and last for 20 years.[119]

---

115   BArch-Koblenz, B 102/240644, Note to TOP 3: "Erdgas-Dreiecksgeschäft", 4 October 1974.

116   BArch-Koblenz, B 102/240644, Telegram from Teheran to Bonn about Natural Gas in Iran, "Lieferverträge mit dem ausland", 20 August 1974.

117   BArch-Koblenz, B 102/163898, Letter to Ms. Dr. Steeg, attachment "Aufzeichung über das Gespräch Bundeskanzler/Ministerpräsident Kossygin vom 29. Oktober 1974 vom 15.00 bis 17.00 Uhr im Kreml", 6 November 1974, fols. 153-155.

118   BStU, MfS HA XVIII 38211, Information Betr. Gasleitungsbau und Gasverteilungsprobleme zwischen SW und NSW in Europa, 14 January 1975, fol. 262.

119   BArch-Koblenz, B 102/240644, Letter from Ruhrgas AG to Dr. Friedrichs regarding Industrial exhibition in Moscow, "Iran/UdSSR/Bundesrepublik

On 30 November 1975, the triangular agreement between the FRG, the USSR and Iran, was eventually signed. It was regarded as one of the most significant energy projects ever and marked the transition from bilateral to multilateral energy agreements.[120]

Graph 9: West German Imports of Soviet gas: amount and value

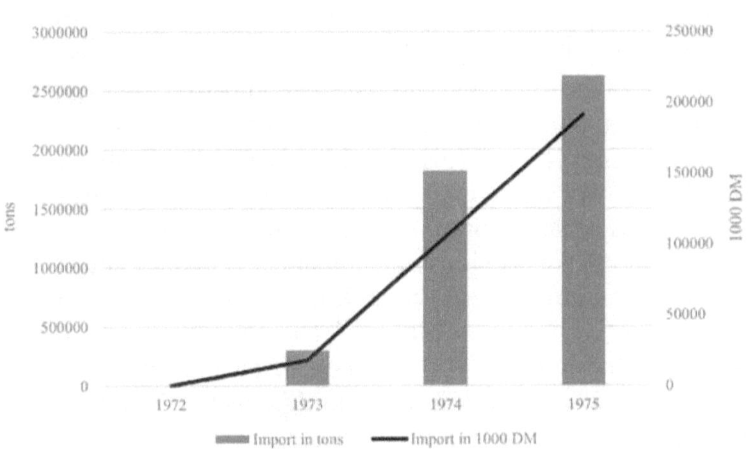

Source: Sowjetunion 1977, p. 139

Following the conclusion of three natural gas agreements and the negotiations of the IGAT II, Schmidt and Otto Wolff von Amerongen continued to pursue a policy of collaboration with other partners. This policy was exemplified by the formation of a joint venture with the Dutch company Nederlandse Aardolie Maatschappij (NAM) and Thyssengas GmbH in April 1976. It regarded the implementation of an agreement concluded in 1966 by NAM and Thyssengas itself for the importation of Dutch natural gas into the FRG.[121] In 1978, Ruhrgas AG[122]

Deutschland", 10 March 1975.

120 Wörmann, xxxviii, pp. 84–85.

121 BArch-Koblenz, B 102/257471, Letter from Thyssengas GmbH to the Federal Office for Trade and Industry regarding Import of Natural Gas from Holland, "Geschäfts-Nr. III 6/08 – 139", 6 April 1976.

122 At the time Ruhrgas AG was the exclusive German Importer of Russian natural gas. Other German companies (companies of Southern Germany

proposed a contract to the USSR in which it would act as the buyer of approximately 8 bcm/y in a consortium with Gaz de France, Gasunie (the Netherlands) and Distrigaz (Belgium). The contract was of particular importance in ensuring the process of energy diversification. Without the new amount of gas from the West, indeed, the proportion of natural gas imports into the FRG from Russia and Iran would have increased from 11% to 22%, potentially reaching a figure of 30%. Consequently, the potential import for other regions could have been utilised to mitigate the impact and maintain the balance of power.[123]

In the same year, during Brezhnev's visit to Bonn, a long-term framework agreement on the development and deepening of Soviet-German economic and industrial cooperation was concluded.[124] Like previous agreements, it called for cooperation in a wide range of areas, including energy development and construction of industrial plants.[125] The agreement was to be in effect for a period of 25 years. The subsequent implementation agreement was signed during Schmidt's visit to Moscow in the summer of 1984.[126]

In general, there was the assumption that trade relations between East and West would (and did) result in the recognition of the political status quo.[127]

Indeed, during the most prosperous period of *Osthandel*, when the FRG had already acknowledged the boundaries of Europe

---

or Thyssengas GmbH and Brigitta Elwerath were trying to extend their independence on Ruhrgas, which, however, continued to hold the monopolio with Russian) – BArch-Koblenz, B 102/257471, Letter from Dr. Engelmann to the Ministry, "Erdgasimporte aus der UdSSR", 24 April 1978.

123 BArch-Koblenz, B 102/257471, Letter from Dr. Engelmann to the Ministry, "Erdgasimporte aus der UdSSR", 24 April 1978.

124 BArch-Koblenz, B 102/257571, Letter of Dr. Wörner on the meeting of the Group of Experts in Moscow at 29.-22.05.1981, Attachment "Übersetzung aus dem Russischen Entwurf des Berichts der Expertengruppe der UdSSR und der BRD über die Zusammenarbeit der beiden Länder aus dem Gebiet der Energiewirtschaft", 1 May 1981.

125 *"Western Europe: Economic Links with the Soviet Bloc". An Intelligence Assessment*, p. 14.

126 Wörmann, xxxviii, p. 54.

127 *Ibid.*, xxxviii, p. 55.

and the division of Germany, there were notable advancements in Western political conduct toward East. Since 1973, the Federal Republic of Germany has entered into a series of agreements with Romania, Hungary, Poland and Czechoslovakia, which were all part of the Soviet-German Cooperation and Détente.[128] Concurrently, Schmidt spearheaded a new phase of German *Ostpolitik*, wherein the relations between the FRG and the Soviet Union reverted to a triangular configuration, with Europe serving as the third vertex instead of the United States.

One of the most significant developments in the "enlarged" *Ostpolitik* in the mid '70s was the Helsinki Final Act of August 1975. The Conference on Security and Cooperation in Europe (CSCE), which commenced on 3 July 1973 and concluded two years later, brought together numerous countries for collaborative discussions. Among the participating nations were the USSR and the USA, which were invited as special guests. They were "motivated by the political will to improve and intensify their relations and to contribute in Europe to peace, security, justice and cooperation as well as to rapprochement among themselves and with the other States of the world".[129] It was composed by four parts:

I.   Questions Relating to Security in Europe. This initial category encompassed general political principles guiding relations between countries and measures of disarmament. Of particular significance were the third and fourth points, inviolability of frontiers and territorial integrity of states, which were analogous to the provisions of the Moscow Treaty and the Basic Agreement. Additionally, the first point, sovereign equality, respect for the rights inherent in sovereignty, assumed that:

> "Within the framework of international law, all the participating States have equal rights and duties. They will respect each other's right to define

---

128 Rudolph, p. 320.
129 'Helsinki Decalogue (1 August 1975)', in *OSCE. Documens 1973-1997* (Vienna: Organization for Security and Cooperation in Europe) <https://www.cvce.eu/obj/helsinki_decalogue_1_august_1975-en-1bccd494-0f57-4816-ad18-6aaba4d73d56.html>.

and conduct as it wishes its relations with other States in accordance with international law and in the spirit of the present Declaration. They consider that their frontiers can be changed, in accordance with international law, by peaceful means and by agreement."[130]

The USSR also demonstrated a willingness to compromise on this matter, although its position on the matter aligns with that of Schiller's Brief to the Moscow Treaty, which aimed to guarantee the possibility of a German reunification.

II. Cooperation in the fields of economics, science and technology, and the environment. This basket was developed based on the concept that:

> "the growing world-wide economic interdependence calls for increasing common and effective efforts towards the solution of major world economic problems such as food, energy, commodities, monetary and financial problems, and therefore emphasizes the need for promoting stable and equitable international economic relations, thus contributing to the continuous and diversified economic development of all countries".[131]

In addition, it dedicates a section to energy, encourages the participation of all countries in projects of common interest in fields of energy resources, in particular petroleum, natural gas and coal, and states that these resources are suitable for strengthening long-term economic cooperation and for the development of trade.

III.   The issue of security and cooperation in the Mediterranean was a complex one, requiring intricate negotiations on behalf of the USSR. These negotiations centred on the question of the free flow of people, the circulation of ideas and information, and the establishment of co-operation within all participating countries, both Mediterranean and non-Mediterranean.

IV.   Follow-up to the Conference.

As Helmut Schmidt observed in his commentary on this treaty, its significance in the history of relations between European countries and others outside the Mediterranean is evident. This was the first instance of a multilateral pact being signed between

---

130   *Ibid.*
131   *Ibid.*

them, rather than a bilateral one, as had been customary in relations with the USSR in the past. Furthermore, he highlighted the status of the city of Berlin, which was finally included in the agreement,[132] although it has already entered into some trade negotiations.

The CSCE conference was of particular significance for Bonn in terms of its relations with the GDR too. As Schmidt asserted in his commentary on the Helsinki Agreement, the borders could only be changed peacefully, and the FRG was committed to working for the reunification of Germany in a détente contest that characterised all of Europe. The reunification could also be viewed as a move to advance Europe as a political entity.[133]

In March 1974, the two Germanies established permanent diplomatic missions in each other's capitals. In September of that same year, East-Berlin removed all mention of the concept of eventual reunification of the two countries from its constitution. Briefly, the Helsinki Final Act reinforced the normalisation of relations between the two countries, which had been initiated at the beginning of the 1970s. This was done from both an economic and a free movement of people perspective.

3.3 *Energy upon ideology*

As already highlighted, in the 1970s, the economic and political situation worldwide presented significant challenges to the combined trade needs and energy supply demands. From the outset of the decade, the dollar and the oil crises, respectively caused by the implications of the Vietnam War on the dollar amount and the subsequent collapse of the dollar standard, as well as the 1973 oil embargo, led to the collapse of the Fordist-Keynesian model. Oil-rich countries were forced to address the

---

132 'Erklärung von Helmut Schmidt (Helsinki, 30. Juli 1975)', in *Bulletin Des Presse- Und Informationsamtes Der Bundesregierung*, 98, Presse- und Informationsamt der Bundesregierung (Bonn: Deutscher Bundesverlag, 1975).

133 *Ibid.*

issue of petrodollars, while Western countries were compelled to combat stagflation.

It is evident that the FRG was also confronted with monetary and financial challenges, as previously outlined. These challenges were not limited to domestic factors, but also extended to the lack of purchasing power among export destinations, including Eastern European countries. Furthermore, they were also exacerbated by new US restrictions on international trade. In the United States, during the Seventies government representatives were becoming increasingly concerned about the close ties between Western Europe and the Soviet Union. Their primary concern was that Moscow was attempting to expand their sphere of influence in Europe through the expansion of machinery and oil and gas trade between the two blocs.[134] In response to the scaling down of investments and limited lending for energy projects by the USA, the USSR revoked the commercial agreements. Washington subsequently initiated measures to limit the export of computer and equipment for the Russian energy industry.

By the end of the decade, the situation had deteriorated further due to a new crisis in the Middle East. In 1978, a revolution erupted in Iran, one of the United States' key allies, leading to a decline in oil production. This disruption may have contributed to a perception of a potential future oil shortage in the West, which in turn exerted pressure on the market price.[135] The crisis created inflationary consequences and exacerbated the petrodollar question for OPEC countries. The price for a barrel of oil reached $30/35.[136] In contrast to the consequences of the

---

134 Ksenia Demidova, 'La Politica degli Stati Uniti nei confronti dell'influenza sovietica sull'Europa Occidentale, 1973-1985', in *La Fine Del Petrolio. Risorse Energetiche e Democrazia Nell'età Contemporanea*, by Elisabetta Bini and Simone Selva (Napoli: L'ancora del Mediterraneo, 2011), p. 111.

135 For a comprehensive examination of the consequences of the events in the Middle East, please refer to Massimo Campanini, *Storia Del Medio Oriente Contemporaneo*, VI (Bologna: Il Mulino, 2006), p. 181 ff. For an overview of the causes and consequences in the energy sector, see Daniel Yergin, *The Prize: The Epic Quest for Oil, Money & Power* (Simon and Schuster, 2011), p. 656 ff.

136 Yergin, *The Prize*, p. 666.

first oil shock, however, Western countries had developed a kind of diversification of energy sources and suppliers, even though they were still largely dependent on Middle Eastern oil.

In addition to the Iranian Revolution, another international political-military action threatened to disrupt German trade relations with Iran and with the Soviet Union: the Soviet intervention in Kabul.

The crisis contributed to a downturn in international trade, characterised by fluctuations in the exchange rates of many Western currencies and a deterioration in the trade balance of Western countries. In an effort to address inflation, unemployment, and irregularities in the energy trade market, the Western Powers enacted measures outlined in the G7 Declarations in June 1979 and June 1980, respectively. At the Tokyo Meeting, strategies previously implemented by Western Industrial countries in mid-1975 were resumed and encouraged, including the promotion of alternative fuels, diversification of suppliers, and reduction of oil consumption.[137] The inability to supply American natural gas, unless through liquefied natural gas (LNG), and the progressive depletion of European energy reserves, along with the unfeasibility of extracting oil in the North Sea due to its high costs, also played a role,[138] and created a favourable condition for a further increase of Soviet market share on European balance of trade. Indeed, the export of energy sources contributed to the growth of Soviet gold reserves, which in turn helped to stabilise the currency and balance of payments. In 1970, these revenues constituted 18.3% of total hard currency earnings, but by 1980, they had risen to 62.3%.[139] Despite the continued dominance of oil as the primary exported fuel, accounting for approximately 50% of Soviet export earnings, the relative growth of natural gas

---

137 La Barca, p. 108.

138 Demidova, 'La Politica degli Stati Uniti nei confronti dell'influenza sovietica sull'Europa Occidentale, 1973-1985', p. 113.

139 Jentleson, From Consensus to Conflict, mentioned in Demidova, 'La Politica degli Stati Uniti nei confronti dell'influenza sovietica sull'Europa Occidentale, 1973-1985', p. 114.

exports reflected the increasing importance of this replacement source among industrial countries.

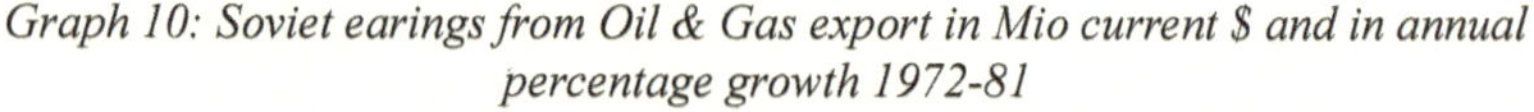

Graph 10: Soviet earings from Oil & Gas export in Mio current $ and in annual percentage growth 1972-81

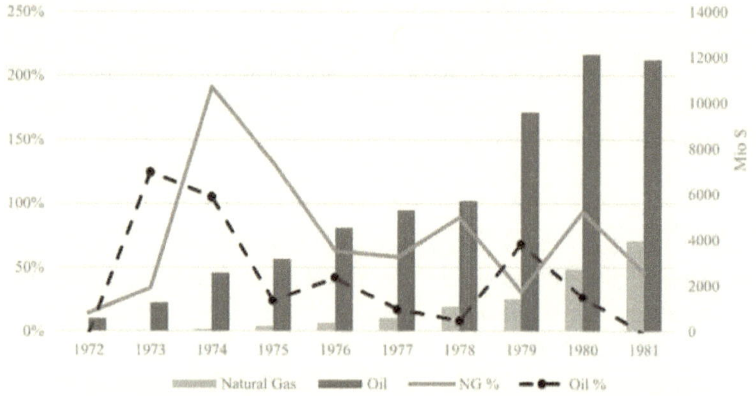

Source: Soviet Energy Data Resource Handbook, CIA Historical Review
Program (Directorate of Intelligence, May 1990), p. 25
<https://www.cia.gov/readingroom/document/0000292332>.

3.3.1 *Energy trade (or) policy*

Despite the complex and multifaceted nature of international politics during the 1970s, which encompassed two oil crises, Soviet interventions in Afghanistan, and the global economic crisis, statistics pertaining to the status of German-Soviet trade at the turn of the decade demonstrated a promising upward trajectory.

At the time, Bonn was engaged in the IGAT II negotiations. Among the German representatives, there was also a sense of unease, with the possibility that the Iranians might not be able to get away with Russian intervention and might inadvertently derail the tripartite agreement.[140] In 1978, the negotiations between

---

140 BArch-Koblenz, B 102/321742, Report of the Embassy of the FRG in
Teheran about the IGAT II/Tripartite Natural Gas Agreement, 13 January

Bonn, Moscow and Tehran continued, despite some challenges. For instance, in April, Tehran had yet to sign two letters of intent with Moss Rosenberg/Norway and Colombia Gas/USA for the delivery of LNG. The project was to be subcontracted by the German joint venture Howaldtswerke-Deutsche Werft/Linde AG.[141] Furthermore, in October, the report on German-Iranian Natural Gas Relations was made public, and Teheran declared its intention to deliver a year after the scheduled date, in 1981. It was also mentioned that negotiations could be held for another supply in the next decade due to a possible decrease in Dutch supplies.[142] However, a year later, Iran ceased the operations of the company Wilmeg, which was indicative of a lack of enthusiasm for the continued implementation of the IGAT II project.[143] Although the Tripartite Agreement was soon cancelled by Iranian Minister of Petroleum Moinfar,[144] this serves to illustrate once more the interdependence of politics and trade.

Moreover, the FRG was not immune to the energy and financial problems affecting global market. At the time, in contrast to the beginning of the 1970s, West Germany had become one of the most industrialised countries in the West, more susceptible than before to energy delivery blockades, and feared the consequences of the second oil shock and the breach of contracts.[145] A briefing paper from the East German Ministry of Security highlighted all the problems with the supply of natural gas and oil to West Germany. The price increase of energy sources was not limited to oil; it also affected natural gas. Bonn

1980.

141 BArch-Koblenz, B 102/321742, Report of the Embassy of the BRD in Teheran, "Flüssiggas (LNG)-Exportprojekte Irans/Interessen deutscher Firmen", 16 May 1978.

142 BArch-Koblenz, B 102/321742, Report of Dr. Pfletschinger and Dr. Ritzmann, "Deutsch- iranische Erdgasbeziehungen", 2 October 1978.

143 BArch-Koblenz, B 102/321742, Iran; Memorandum der Fa. Borsig vom 25.7.1979, 6 August 1979.

144 BArch-Koblenz, B 102/321742, Telegram from Teheran to Bonn about the Iranian foreign policy-IGAT II/I, 4 February 1980.

145 For further details, please refer to Michael J. Sodaro, *Moscow, Germany, and the West from Khrushev to Gorbachev* (London: I.B. Tauris, 1991), pp. 266–83.

was obliged to accommodate higher price demands from Dutch natural gas suppliers, which had already been implemented against Austria and Italy. As Ruhrgas AG Hey had no domestic reserves, it was necessary to make a significant amount of capital available to it in the following years for participation in the production and utilisation of natural gas and oil abroad, including in the United States, as well as in the development of Norwegian fields and in projects with Algeria. It is important to note, however, that the project with Algeria was not considered politically safe. Furthermore, the logistics of transporting liquefied gas to Europe were unclear, as the construction of a gas pipeline by a consortium of Western European energy companies, despite being the most economically favourable option, also posed significant risks. The Algerian government was increasingly transforming the economic agreement into a political issue, with the intention of achieving national political and economic goals. This resulted in the agreement with the Federal Republic and Western Europe becoming increasingly vague.[146]

The breakdown of the IGAT II did not result in a deterioration of relations with Moscow, which was now more than ever seen as a stable market to rely on. Germany considered Russia the world's largest energy fuels producer and a relatively secure country, as a potential substitute for the long-term loss of Iranian commodities. In 1980, the exchange of goods between the Federal Republic of Germany and the Union of Soviet Socialist Republics reached 9.8%. This rate doubled between 1976 and 1980 in comparison to the period 1971-1975. German exports to the USSR had a positive impact on such an increase. In contrast to the 1976 period, when a considerable amount of Soviet imports were registered in the FRG, in 1980 German exports to the Warsaw Pact countries

---

146   Bundesarchiv – Stasi Unterlagen Archiv (BStU), MfS, HA XVIII /38211, Information über Probleme der Erdöl- und Erdgasversorgung der BRD, Streng geheim!, 11 February 1980, fols. 65-67.

reached 19%, which was a higher figure than the total amount of German exports worldwide.[147]

The composition of Soviet imports exhibited particular characteristics. As previously documented, a close collaboration between Moscow and Bonn was established during the 1970s, facilitated by a partnership between Sojuzgazexport and Ruhrgas AG. This partnership was instrumental in the construction of infrastructure for the delivery of natural gas from the USSR to the FRG. Schmidt was even more compelled to safeguard the energy supply of his country and to guarantee energy security using the new roots. At a later point in time, Germany revised its energy programme, which incorporated a greater quantity of gas imports than oil. This was in accordance with the slogan "weg vom Öl" (literally, "away from oil"), which was also a departure from the Middle East.[148] The trend of increasing gas imports was consistent with the broader trends observed in the German energy market. Both oil and natural gas imports exhibited a steady and upward trajectory, respectively. Approximately 80% of Soviet exports to the FRG consisted of energy fuels, namely crude oil, oil products and natural gas. In comparison to the previous year, West Germany exhibited a decline in the importation of Soviet oil products and crude oil, respectively, by 51% and 21%. Conversely, the delivery of natural gas exhibited a consistent upward trajectory, increasing by 13%. Nevertheless, the USSR registered additional income of DM 2 billion, attributable to the price increase for all energy fuels, with the price of oil products increasing by 135%, crude oil by 68%, and natural gas by 65%.[149]

---

147 BArch-Koblenz, B 102/234235, Tagesordnung der Tagung der Arbeitsgruppe der Kommission der Bundesrepublik Deutschland und der Union der Sozialistischen Sowjetrepubliken für wirtschaftliche und wissenschaftlich-technische Zusammenarbeit, Moskau, 26-28 January 1981.

148 Gross, 'Making Space for Sanctions', p 4.

149 BArch-Koblenz, B 102/234235, Tagesordnung der Tagung der Arbeitsgruppe der Kommission der Bundesrepublik Deutschland und der Union der Sozialistischen Sowjetrepubliken für wirtschaftliche und wissenschaftlich-technische Zusammenarbeit, Moskau, 26-28 January 1981.

Graph 11: FRG Natural Gas Imports per Suppliers in percentage rate 1972-81

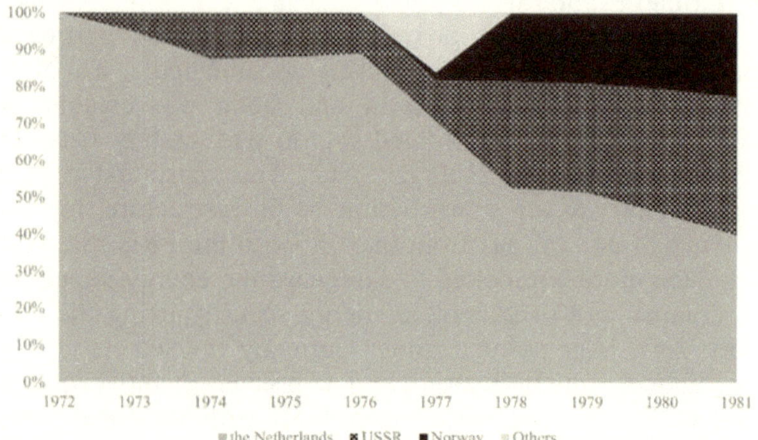

Source: 'Entwicklung des deutschen Gasmarktes (monatliche Bilanz 1998 –
2017, Einfuhr seit 1960)' (BAFA) <https://www.bafa.de/SharedDocs/Downloads/
DE/Energie/egas_entwicklung_1991.html>.

Nevertheless, despite the growing reliance on Soviet energy
imports, the proportion of the USSR in German energy
consumption remained relatively low in comparison with other
importers, at 5.4%. The dependence on OPEC was 29%, while
the one on Arabian countries was 24.9%.[150] The data indicate,
however, that the USSR was actually increasing its importance in
the European and particularly West-German market, since it was
not considered a significant threat to German energy security.
But its share of the market was, however, maintained relatively
low, so a potential disruption from its fields would not have a
significant impact on energy provision.

The FRG's objective in these years was to consolidate this
supply market. Schmidt, representing a consortium comprising
Ruhrgas AG, Mannesmann, Siemens and Deutsche Bank, instead
proceeded to Moscow to negotiate a further trade agreement

---

150 BArch-Koblenz, B 102/257569, Table 3 "Importabhängigkeit der
Energieversorgung der Bundesrepublik Deutschland von wichtigen Öl- und
Gaslieferländern im Jahre 1980", October 1980.

with Brezhnev. The objective was to secure additional energy sources for the country and for other European industrial nations. Moscow at the time of the crisis was engaged in another ongoing negotiation with the key Western countries (FRG, France, Italy and the United Kingdom) for the construction of a new natural gas pipeline, the Siberian Natural Gas Pipeline (SNGP). The project was regarded in Europe as the "deal of the century", as it would represent a pioneering initiative in the global energy sector.[151] The project advocated for:

–   A pipeline extended approximately 4,500 km;

–   A delivery of approximately 45 billion cubic metres of natural gas per year. Of these, 30 billion cubic metres would be delivered to the Western Consortium, comprising Ruhrgas, Gaz de France, Gasunie, and Distrigaz. The remaining 10 to 12 billion cubic metres would be delivered to the Federal Republic of Germany. Other buyers included Sweden, Switzerland, and Spain;

–   The delivery would commence in 1984 or 1985 and would last for 25 years.[152]

–   The pipeline would have 42 compressor stations along its route, with the gas being pumped from the Urengoy gas field in Russia to Central and Western European countries via Uzhgorod in Western Ukraine.[153]

The opening of the Urengoy Pipeline would facilitate the expansion of trade between West Berlin and the German Democratic Republic, particularly in light of the ongoing debate surrounding the transit question. From the outset of the negotiations, Dieter Von Würzen, the head of Department IV of the Federal Ministry for Economic Affairs (Commercial Economy/ Economic Development Berlin), had highlighted the financial

---

151 Demidova, 'La Politica degli Stati Uniti nei confronti dell'influenza sovietica sull'Europa Occidentale, 1973-1985', p. 114.

152 BArch-Koblenz, B 122/8526, Information note of Dr. Ritzmann, "Gespräh mit der Fa. Mannesmann am 15. April 1980 über ein neues Erdgas-Röhren-Geschäft mit der UdSSR", 11 April 1980.

153 Phillip Freiberg, 'Reagan Administration and the Soviet Pipeline Embargo', 2011, p. 5 <https://doi.org/10.13140/2.1.1340.0964>.

implications of such an agreement, the political instability that it would exacerbate, the potential for German dependence on the Soviets to increase, and so forth.[154] In particular, concerns were raised regarding the last point, given that the Russian share in German natural gas imports was projected to reach 30%. However, it was argued that West Germany should have become dependent on Soviet reserves only when the imported quota exceeded 30%.[155]

A long-term agreement between the USSR and Western countries could have significant benefits for both parties. For the USSR, it would provide a reliable source of foreign currency, while for Western countries, it would reduce the risk of disruption in the supply chain.[156]

Furthermore, the project could benefit not only energy demand but also German companies, thereby contributing to German economic wealth. One of the companies that played a significant role in the project was Ruhrgas AG. It was responsible for the transit of Russian natural gas through the FRG to other European countries, as well as for all matters pertaining to the distribution of that commodity in the European market.[157] Another German industrial enterprise with a strong presence in the steel and industrial sectors, Mannesmann AG, was also involved in the project. In addition to pipes, the company expressed interest in selling higher-tech goods to be used in pumping stations.[158]

---

154 BArch-Koblenz, B 102/257563, Report of Dr. Pfletschinger regarding Natural Gas Import from the USSR, "Gespräch Mannesmann (Bering, van Beveren) bei StS Dr. Von Würzen am 15.04.1980", 21 April 1980.

155 BArch-Koblenz, B 102/257565, Report of Dr. Pfletschinger on the new Natural Gas/Pipes trade with the USSR, "Höflichkeitsbesuch von Minister Ossipov bei StS. Dr. Schlecht am 23. September 1980 im BMWi", 23 September 1980.

156 BArch-Koblenz, B 102/257563, Recording of the BfW, "Voraussichtliche Entwicklung der deutschen Erdgasimporte, insbesondere aus der Sowjetunion", 24 April 1980.

157 BArch-Koblenz, B 102/257565, Memorandum of Ruhrgas AG regarding the new Natural Gas Export Project, 12 August 1980.

158 BArch-Koblenz, B 102/257563, Report of Dr. Pfletschinger regarding Natural Gas Import from the USSR, "Gespräch Mannesmann (Bering, van Beveren) bei StS Dr. Von Würzen am 15.04.1980", 21 April 1980.

The company provided an order of DM 5.5 billion in 1981-1983, representing approximately 28% of the total German exports to the USSR.[159] As a preliminary to the conclusion of the negotiations, Mannesmann was prepared to offer a 100% financing of export credits.[160]

In addition to the planned 'gas pipeline deal', in 1980 West Germany was also pursuing other talks on a supplementary agreement between Moscow and Bonn, which would guarantee Western gas companies, particularly Ruhrgas AG, an additional 40 bcm of gas per year from the USSR from 1985 in return for pipeline pipes worth around 15 billion DM. These were to be supplied by a consortium of French, Dutch and West German companies led by Mannesmann AG.[161] In addition to Mannesmann, other industrialised Western countries would offer not only technology for the infrastructure but also loans with a low interest rate for the purchase of materials and equipment in exchange for future Soviet low-cost gas deliveries. The Deutsche Bank, as the lead manager of the consortium managing the financial issues, offered the Soviet Foreign Trade Minister Ivanov a finance volume of DM 10 billion for 10 years and an interest rate of 7.75%.[162]

In consideration of the total volume of investment from the West, it was agreed that an investment of $1,130 million would be made in the project, with the objective of supplying steel for pipes and compressor stations. In return, the West would receive 370 billion cubic feet of gas per year at a price of $4.60-$4.90 per thousand cubic feet.[163]

---

159 BArch-Koblenz, B 102/257563, Recording of the BfW, "Voraussichtliche Entwicklung der deutschen Erdgasimporte, insbesondere aus der Sowjetunion", 24 April 1980.

160 BArch-Koblenz, B 102/257565, Memorandum of Mannesmann AG regarding Russian Business VI (Yamal-Project), 12 August 1980.

161 BStU, MfS, HA XVIII/38211, Information G/3641/04/07/80, Streng vertraulich, fol. 4.

162 BArch-Koblenz, B 102/257569, Report regarding the citizenship policy throughout the Soviet Union, "Erdgasröhrenprojekt", 17 November 1980.

163 Demidova, 'The Deal of the Century: The Reagan Administration and the Soviet Pipeline', p. 62.

3.3.2 *Trade War?*

The negotiation process for the new natural gas agreement, however, spanned a considerable period of time, as it gave rise to an international diplomatic dispute between the FRG, the USSR and also other European countries on the one side and the United States on the other one.

While in Europe the idea was established that the Soviet Union was a necessary target and an essential supply market for energy products in particular, since the Middle East, after its shocks, was considered unsafe, and moreover was a profitable and lucrative outlet for European states, the United States continued to view European policy, including energy and economic policy, as a weapon to be used as blackmail against Moscow's peceived aggressive policies.[164]

Americans condemned Soviet intervention in Afghanistan and yet President Carter had insisted on punishing the USSR with a grain embargo.[165] This was not the sole restriction imposed on trade with the USSR by Americans in the late 1970s and early 1980s. Jimmy Carter, in charge as US President since 1977, played a pivotal role in the conflict over trade and détente with the East. As Schmidt openly states, he hindered European and specifically West-German interests.[166] Lippert points out that Carter, perhaps more than his predecessors, dealt with crises only in terms of how they might affect the US, without taking the allies in Western Europe into account at all.[167] In 1978, he supported the Technology Transfer Ban Act: export of computers and related equipment to the Soviet energy industry was restricted as well as export of high-tech items for oil and gas deliveries. He asserted the necessity of a "valid license" for the export of all

---

164 For an overview of the evolution of relations between the United States and Europe concerning the embargoes against the Soviet Union, please refer to the following source: Engels and Schwartz.

165 Lippert, 'European Long-Term Investments in Détente', p. 89; Jüngerkes, p. 249.

166 Schmidt, p. 127.

167 Lippert, 'European Long-Term Investments in Détente', p. 88.

goods required by the Soviets for oil exploration, transportation, or production. In this manner, trade with the East would be guaranteed only for the achievement of American foreign policy objectives.[168] Initially, these measures did not constitute outright prohibitions. However, they established the foundation for a political instrumentalisation of American exports to the USSR. All of these procedures anticipated and paved the way for the Reagan Administration's sanctions against pipelines in 1979.[169]

The initial grain embargo had a detrimental impact on American industry, so later Reagan, Carter's successor, was reluctant to impose another restriction that could be proved to be more detrimental to the US than to the Soviets.[170] Consequently, the second embargo was drawn up with regard to the energy sector and involved equipment to be used in energy industry, and instead, the new negotiations on the energy sector between Europe and Moscow.[171] The growing volume of natural gas imports from the USSR to the FRG and subsequently to other European countries, coupled with the construction of a more extensive and sophisticated energy grid and infrastructure in Europe, prompted concern in the United States. In the US' perception, the technical expertise and technology transferred from Western Europe to the Soviet Union for the purpose of enhancing and modernising energy infrastructure were employed to facilitate the production and technical sophistication of weaponry, by expanding industries for military production and in general by alleviating economic challenges (principally for improving hard currency reserves). In reality, Soviet hard currency imports played a pivotal role in numerous industrial, agricultural, energy and military programmes themselves, as well as for procuring the necessary materials for these projects.[172] Russian government allocated the majority of its resources to the arms industry, with the military industry receiving the most significant share of

---

168 Mastanduno, pp. 153–56; 206–8.
169 Engels and Schwartz, pp. 234–35; Wörmann, xxxviii, pp. 42–47.
170 Freiberg, p. 6.
171 Mastanduno, p. 223.
172 The Soviet Gas Pipeline in Perspective, CIA.

funding for machine tools and instruments. Furthermore, the industry was the primary beneficiary of innovation.[173] With the embargo, the intention was therefore the same as the one behind the embargo on large-diameter pipes in the 1960s: if not to block, then at least to slow down the Soviet Union's expansion into the European market.

Should European powers have acquiesced to US decisions, this would have resulted in a significant delay to energy projects with Russia, as perceived by Reagan, and it would have had the effect of weakening the Soviet foreign trade trend. However, Reagan's analysis failed to take into account the potential implications for European energy security policy. Such a measure would not only have negatively impacted the economic and trade relationship between the USSR and the West, but would also have undermined European energy policy, which is based on the principle that "the more Europe diversifies its imports, the greater its security supply" and industrial trade. The trade of machinery for specialized oil exploration, pipes, drilling, pumping and processing equipment was a trade that the USSR had traditionally conducted with Western European countries and Japan. The embargo would have been unsuccessful in the absence of the support of European countries.[174] Washington, however, was unaware that not only Moscow or Western industries, but also Western banks, derived benefits from energy trade. The sale of energy fuel increased Soviet foreign currency reserves, which the USSR used to repay debts with Western banks, including the German ones.

To get the embargo accepted, it was also suggested that too much dependence on the USSR was becoming dangerous. In any case, European countries were aware of the potential dependence on the USSR for natural gas supply. Before definitively signing the agreement, they conducted their own studies on the future implications of such an agreement on their economy and energy

---

173 Hannes Adomeit, *Imperial Overstretch. Germany in Soviet Policy from Stalin to Gorbachev*, 2° (Baden-Baden: Nomos, 2016), pp. 178–79.
174 Demidova, 'La Politica degli Stati Uniti nei confronti dell'influenza sovietica sull'Europa Occidentale, 1973-1985', p. 116.

security. The most involved representatives in the "big deal" – West Germany and France – settled a long debate on the effective danger of the trade with the USSR. One of the initial points highlighted in the talks between the German and French delegations was the mutual significance of the agreement for both the Eastern and Western blocs. While European countries (EC and IEA) were attempting to diversify their energy supply, the USSR exploited the collaboration for financial and technological gain. Consequently, the Soviet Union too became dependent on EC, which mitigated the risk of Moscow abruptly terminating or cancelling the framework.[175] Moreover, statistical forecasts concerning the proportion of natural gas in national energy consumption indicated that, by 1990 (approximately six years after the commencement of deliveries via the SNGP), the total Soviet gas (including the gas transported via previous pipelines) would account for 31% of the total gas supply in the FRG and 27-31% in France. Furthermore, it was predicted that the combined share of natural gas in the total energy mix in the FRG and France would reach 31% and 27-31%, respectively, by 1980. This would represent a significant increase from respectively the 18% and 12% observed in 1980. It is also important to consider the situation in West Germany. In 1990, the share of internal or European supply of natural gas would have been only 11% lower than in 1980. This represented a relatively modest decrease, with the share of natural gas in total energy use remaining at a high level of 61%. In contrast, the share of natural gas supplied by the Soviet Union was calculated to be only 5-6% of total energy use.[176] Moreover, it was guaranteed that the FRG would serve as a transit country, and it was also possible that it would transit through the CSSR. The project was, in that case, considered

---

175 BArch-Koblenz, B 102/257569, Letter from the Federal Foreign Office to the Federal Minister of Economy regarding the Natural Gas/Pipes business with the Soviet Union, Attachment "Außenpolitische Überlegungen zur Diskussion über mögliche Gefahren der Abhängigkeit auf Grund des Erdgasröhrengeschäfte mit der SU", 18 February 1981.
176 BArch-Koblenz, B 102/257569, Stichworte, Deutsch-französische Konsultationen über UdSSR-Gas am 20. Februar 1981 in Bonn.

secure because the establishment of this 'common' network would preclude the occurrence of a supply interruption affecting only a single country.[177]

At the beginning of 1981, rumours were still circulating in Europe about the concrete possibility of American official measures against the proposed deal. Since the negotiations were still in progress – the green light for the project had been given in May 1980 – it was said that Washington would engage with NATO to ensure the unsuccessfulness of the negotiations. In that period, the Consortium for financing the project had to close the contract. The signing was postponed, since the German Foreign Minister, Hans-Dietrich Genscher, and the German Defence Minister, Hans-Joachim von Merkatz, were dispatched to Washington to forestall any involvement of NATO.[178] It is clear that Reagan was aware of the European reluctance to impose restrictions on any financial or commercial dealings. Indeed, he attempted to persuade his allies of the Soviet military threat in any way possible. At the NATO Conference in Rome in May 1981, the Council of Ministers agreed that:

> "The strength and cohesion of the Alliance remain indispensable to guarantee the security of its members and thereby to foster stable international relations. [...] Claims by the Soviet Union that it too subscribes to such policies are not borne out by Soviet deeds. The more constructive East-West relationship which the Allies seek requires tangible signs that the Soviet Union is prepared to abandon the disturbing build-up of its military strength, to desist from resorting to force and intimidation and to cease creating or exploiting situations of crisis and instability in the Third World. [...] The Soviet invasion and occupation of Afghanistan is a particularly flagrant example of violation of the principles of restraint and responsibility in international affairs. [...]

---

177 BArch-Koblenz, B 102/257569, Letter of Dr. Engelmann regarding the talking with the Federal Chancellor about the new Natural Gas/Pipes business with the USSR on 23.02.1981, Attachment "Sprechzettel: Gespräch mit dem Bundeskanzler am 23. Februar 1981 über das neue Erdgas-Röhren-Geschäft mit der UdSSR".

178 *Ibid.*

> In Europe, efforts to restore East-West co-operation and exchanges on the basis of the Helsinki Final Act cannot but be severely undermined by the use or threat of force for intervention in the affairs of other countries. Poland must be left free to resolve its own problems. Any outside intervention would have the gravest consequences for international relations as a whole and would fundamentally change the entire international situation. [...] In Europe, efforts to restore East-West co-operation and exchanges on the basis of the Helsinki Final Act cannot but be severely undermined by the use or threat of force for intervention in the affairs of other countries."[179]

Following these events, there were several discussions between German and Soviet representatives. In one of the first speeches after the visit to Washington, Graff Lambardoff asserted that the FRG would support the trade despite American criticism and would guarantee the loans. However, the companies were required to negotiate the specifics of the agreement, as the state itself was not directly involved.[180]

Consequently, Reagan leveraged his position within the CoCom to advance a different course of action. At the Natural Security Council meeting in July 1981, the US and other participants agreed to the control of all military-relevant technology, including oil and gas equipment and technology export to the Soviet Union. One of the consequences of the imposition of this control was that the US company Caterpillar was denied an export licence for the delivery of pipe-layers to the USSR to be used on the Urengoy project.[181] To exert pressure on European countries, and in consideration of the significant threat to its military security and the need to avoid undue interference with its allies across the Atlantic, Schmidt had indicated his willingness to temporary accept a CoCom directive.[182]

---

179 Joseph Luns, 'NATO Council, Rome 4th-5th May, 1981. Final Communiqué.', NATO Online Library <https://www.nato.int/docu/comm/49-95/c810504a.htm>.

180 BArch-Koblenz, B 102/257571, Bericht über das Gespräch des Bundeswirtschaftsministers mit dem Präsidenten der sowjetischen Gosbank, Alchimow, am 4. Juni 1981.

181 Demidova, 'The Deal of the Century: The Reagan Administration and the Soviet Pipeline', p. 63.

182 Jüngerkes, pp. 49–50.

Nevertheless, this measure did not impede Germany's continued engagement in negotiations with the USSR. One of the objectives of the FRG was also to facilitate the inclusion of West Berlin in the agreement, with a supply of approximately 1 bcm of Soviet natural gas per year. There were several potential avenues to deliver gas to West Berlin, including through the newly constructed pipelines network with the USSR or through the GDR.[183] In July, Ruhrgas AG formalised with Sojuzgazexport the request for the inclusion of West Berlin in the agreement and the possibility of involving the GRD in the supply.[184] On 20 November 1981, the contract for the delivery of 10.5 bcm/y to the FRG and 0.7 bcm/y to West Berlin over a 25-year period, commencing in 1984, was signed. It was also observed that the political effects on the USSR of such an agreement would be diluted by the fact that the gas deal was embedded in a multilateral Western European framework. The inclusion of West Berlin in the deal was of essential importance. From a political perspective, a more stable outlook for the city would diminish the potential risk of a supply blockade, as was the case in 1948. At the same time, it limited the scope for Soviet attempts to use the country's gas supply position as a political leverage, because any attempt to cut gas export would have an impact not only on countries involved directly in the framework but also on the Three Allied Powers, including the US.[185]

The project continued to be the subject of criticism in the USA, with concerns that Moscow might emerge as a more powerful global force than Washington. The senators responsible for energy began to consider ways to avoid the project.

---

183 BArch-Koblenz, B 102/234235, Information note of Dr. Schäfer regarding Energy supply of Berlin, "Energieprojekte mit der DDR und UdSSR", 1 September 1981.

184 BArch-Koblenz, B 102/234235, Ausführungen von Staatssekretär Dr. von Würzen gegenüber Minister Sölle zum Thema Erdgas für das Leipziger Gespräch am 8. September 1981.

185 BArch-Koblenz, B 102/257577, Report of the International Energy Agency, "Some Aspects of Soviet Gas Exports to Western Europe", 10 December 1981.

The final straw which prompted a series of American positions against the USSR and the SNGP was the establishment of martial law in Poland on December 13, 1981. This was intended to suppress the political opposition against the Communist government. The intervention contravened the position previously articulated at the NATO Conference in May, namely that Poland should be permitted to resolve its own problems. It also afforded the Allies the opportunity to take international measures. On 30 December, the US Administration, among other things, imposed an embargo on the export of all gas and oil equipment and technology produced in the US to be exported to the Soviet Union.[186] On another occasion, the measures did not apply to the grain field, thus avoiding any potential harm to American trade. All Western counties condemned the Polish situation and Communist actions, yet they did not support the embargo policy. The prohibition had an impact on several American companies that had entered into contracts with German industries, even in cases where the contracts had been concluded retroactively. For instance, General Electric supplied AEG, a German company that had been involved in the supply of gas turbines to the USSR as part of the Urengoy agreement, with single elements.[187] Mannesmann continued to sign agreements with the Soviets for pipe orders.[188] At the same time, Caterpillar and Komatsu too, reslectively an American and a Japanaise company, on the other hand, supplied pipe-layers.[189]

The decision to suspend the disruption of licensed production supplying German and other Western European industrial companies involved in the construction of the gas pipeline was, nevertheless, taken. This measure would have a detrimental effect

---

186 Demidova, 'The Deal of the Century: The Reagan Administration and the Soviet Pipeline', p. 66.

187 BArch-Koblenz, B 102/257577, Note about the involvment of AEG in the Natural Gas- Pipeline.Project West-Siberia – Europe, "Auswirkungen eventueller amerikanischer Embargo- Maßnahmen (Erklärung von Präsident Reagan vom 29. Dezember 1981), 30 December 1981.

188 Lippert, 'European Long-Term Investments in Détente', pp. 91–92.

189 BArch-Koblenz, B 102/257577, Memorandum about the US-Sanctions against the USSR, Bonn, 30 December 1981

on the USSR and transatlantic industrial co-operation in the long term.[190] Western European countries eventually approved the establishment of a special committee to monitor technology transfer and agreed to enhance transparency in trade relations, with the intention of implementing a list of technology and equipment that would be prohibited for export to the USSR.[191] However, tensions between Western European countries, in particular France, the FRG and the UK, and the USA persisted for several months in a sanctions-refuses battle. It is important to note that this 'trade conflict', in addition to other critical elements influencing the economic sector, resulted in an economic crisis on both sides of the Atlantic. The global economic recession led to a decline in sales, the emergence of protectionist tendencies, and the impact of the crisis on various economic sectors, including agriculture and the steel trade. Moreover, the crisis had to address financial aspects, including high interest rates, the instability of the dollar, and the rise in public debt.[192]

By the end of June, the Reagan administration had reached an impasse in its negotiations with the EC. In response, the administration implemented a new national export restriction policy, citing "foreign policy issues" as the rationale. Notably, this policy diverged from the Export Administration Act, which had previously governed the controls on export based on security policy.[193] It was prohibited for individuals in a third country to reexport machinery for the exploration, production, transmission, or refinement of oil and natural gas, or components thereof, if it was of US origin, without the permission of the US government.[194] As foretold by the Chancellor Schmidt, this decision led to a significant disruption in international trade, not only between the Western and Eastern Bloc, but also among

---

190 BArch-Koblenz, B 136/17817, Telegram from Chancellor Schmidt to Us President Reagan, Translation, 5 March 1982
191 Demidova, 'The Deal of the Century: The Reagan Administration and the Soviet Pipeline', p. 76.
192 Wörmann, xxxviii, pp. 153–54.
193 *Ibid.*, xxxviii, p. 157.
194 Demidova, 'La Politica degli Stati Uniti nei confronti dell'influenza sovietica sull'Europa Occidentale, 1973-1985', p. 123.

Western countries themselves, and in particular in transatlantic relations, both in the near term and for the long term.

Indeed, there were several arguments against the extended embargo. These included the underestimated potential indirect effects, such as the possibility that European business would not enter into marketing, which could be derailed by unilateral political decisions. Furthermore, the extended embargo would have a negative impact on US efforts to extend the GATT agreements to cover trade in services, investments and high technology. Finally, the extended embargo would violate the principles of free trade and free market economy.[195]

The American restrictions and imposition were in contrast with international law, in particular with the principles of territoriality and nationality. The measures sought to regulate companies not of US nationality outside the USA and to impose on them the restrictions of American law by threatening them with discriminatory sanctions in the field of trade, which were inconsistent with the normal commercial practice established between the USA and the EC.[196]

Reagan also insisted on financial issues in his opposition to the SNGP agreement. He demanded the reduction of guarantees on credits for exporting. Without these guarantees, German banks would have been unable to provide long-term loans for the expansion and support of heavy industry in projects with the Soviets.

Furthermore, the refusal of Hermes to provide loans could have allowed the USSR to initiate legal proceedings.[197] In July, the German Bank Consortium and the Soviet Foreign Bank terminated the credit agreement with a loan interest rate of 7.8% and an effective interest rate of 11.2%.[198] The discrepancy

---

195 BArch-Koblenz, B 136/17817, Copy of the letter of American Chamber of Commerce in Germany to US President Reagan, 15 July 1982.

196 BArch-Koblenz, B 136/17817, Kommentar der Europäischen Gemeinschaft zu dem am 22. Juni 1982 zu den US-Ausfuhrvorschriften verkündeten "Amendments", 10 August 1982.

197 Jüngerkes, pp. 249–50.

198 BArch-Koblenz, B 136/17817, Memorandum about the financing of the German equipment purchases regarding the Natural Gas business with the USSR through German Banks, 19 July 1982.

between the two rates was offset by a lower gas price charged by the USSR and by higher prices of German goods supplied for the construction of the pipeline. In response to pressure of Reagan, the OECD agreed to include the USSR, the FRG and other Eastern countries in the group of 'relative rich countries'. This could result in an increase of approximately 50% in the minimum interest rates for credits to the USSR, from 8.25% to 12.15%, and a reduction in the maturities from 8 to 5 years. In this way, the FRG and other countries sought to condemn the events in Poland while opposing the embargo.[199]

According to Western European countries, the Soviet gas deal still was advantageous in terms of security, flexibility and price. These incentives, as evidenced by several CIA Intelligence reports on the Soviet Pipeline, were a key factor in shaping the political and strategic considerations of these countries. Firstly, the gas pipeline had to provide West Europeans with a 25-year gas supply from a partner more reliable than OPEC. Secondly, the contract was significant flexible: the Western parts could reduce every year the supply quote. The price too was cheaper than the common market.[200] There were also other consideration: the desire to restore the détente climate, to maintain access to Eastern Europe, and the belief that such relations could positively influence Soviet behaviour in the future.[201]

Western European reluctance toward US behaviour was further compounded by the uninterrupted export of US grain to the Soviet Union. The British government prohibited its companies from complying with the US embargo, yet German representatives were unable to do the same and instead urged the

---

199 BArch-Koblenz, B 136/17817, Article of Otto G. Lambsdorff, *"The German Case for the Pipeline"*, Washington Post, 28 July 1982.

200 CIA, *"Western Europe: Economic Links with the Soviet Bloc"* -An Intelligence Assessment, 05.1983.

201 *The Soviet Gas Pipeline in Perspective* (Directorate of Intelligence, 17 September 1982) <https://www.cia.gov/readingroom/document/cia-rdp88b00443r001203970095-9>.

companies not to respect the sanctions, given that the FRG did not have the British Protection of Trading Interests Act.[202]

As Engels and Schwartz posit, the situation in 1982 was distinct from that of the previous decade, primarily due to a shift in the perception of danger. In contrast to the similarly situation of the 1960s, when the memory of the Wall and Cuba was still fresh in the minds of the German people and the contrast between the GDR and the Federal Republic of Germany was stark, the German government in the 1980s did not perceive Soviet actions as direct threats to West Berlin or West German territory. Instead, they were regarded as internal affairs of the Warsaw Pact.[203] Although this is objectively accurate, it is important to consider the relevant economic factors that influenced the outcome. These factors may be summarised as follows:

I.   In the 1960s, particularly in the early years, there was not yet a significant issue with energy diversification, and there was still a strong reliance on coal as the primary domestic source. Moreover, the United States' dominance in oil production, exemplified by the Seven Sisters, was still considerable, and therefore, the end of Soviet gas or oil imports did not have the same profound impact on the economy as it would have in the 1980s.

II.   The necessity of ensuring a reliable and stable import of energy, mitigating the risk of energy supply diversification, as previously outlined. One strategy to achieve this was to maintain relations with the USSR, which was perceived as a less volatile partner than OPEC producers.

III.   The significant internal economic downturn. By 1980, Germany was facing a recession, and the only prospect for future growth was foreign trade.

IV.   Germany's significant industrial sectors, including lathes and pressurised pipelines, were heavily involved in the construction of the SNGP mega project. This presented an

---

202 BArch-Koblenz, B 136/17817, Letter of Dr. Marx about the US Sanctions against the USSR, "Voraussichtliches Verhalten der deutschen Unternehmen und weiteres Vorgehen der Bundesregierung", 6 August 1982.

203 Engels and Schwartz, p. 241; Wörmann, xxxviii, p. 142.

opportunity for these industries to reinvigorate their foreign sales following the period of crisis.[204]

In summary, the situation at the beginning of '80s resembled the one of 1962/63 after the *Röhrenembargo*, with the difference that now the FRG had sided with other European countries and refused American unilateral imposition to the detriment of its trade. However, the USA did not expect that behaviour from Germany, they thought "the West Germany will be reluctant to proceed with the pipeline deal in the face of a mounting consensus opposing it."[205]

While the European Allies required several years to lift the embargo in the 1960s, the process was completed in just a few months in 1982. In November of that year, Reagan lifted the sanctions, and in exchange, the Europeans agreed to participate in OECD, NATO and Cocom studies on energy trends. Though, they were not required to follow the recommendations. In general, the USA was unable to persuade its European allies to comply with its strategy of achieving political objectives through economic means.[206]

3.4 *Towards the Unification*

In 1983, the SPD-FDP government, led by Helmut Schmidt, collapsed as a consequence of internal party disputes surrounding the deployment of the INF (Intermediate-Range Nuclear Forces). At the subsequent election in March, the CDU/CSU-FDP coalition government, led by Helmut Kohl, assumed power.[207] This could potentially re-establish the FRG's connection to the USA following the "trade war". However, only a few months after the lifting of sanctions and amendments in Washington, a

---

204 Gross, 'Making Space for Sanctions', pp. 7–12.
205 Demidova, 'The Deal of the Century: The Reagan Administration and the Soviet Pipeline', p. 73.
206 Demidova, 'La Politica degli Stati Uniti nei confronti dell'influenza sovietica sull'Europa Occidentale, 1973-1985', pp. 124–25.
207 Adomeit, p. 164.

second act was initiated. In May 1983, a proposal was made that Western Europe could adopt restrictions on energy equipment, technology and know-how.[208] Although Kohl was inclined to follow the lead of the United States, he was a staunch proponent of trade with the Communist bloc and strongly invoked the past success of Soviet-German commercial relations, acting against United States' request.

In contrast with Helmut Schmidt, Kohl emphasised the significance of NATO security considerations in FRG-Soviet trade. Furthermore, he asserted that Bonn would continue its economic relations with Moscow on the basis of the Harmal Report, signed in 1967,[209] the Bonn Declaration of the Alliance and the Versailles economic summit (both June 1982).[210] The common thread between these documents was the peacekeeping and cooperation between the two sides, the attention to mutual welfare and advantage from political and economic measures, the importance of the Four Allies in Berlin for maintaining peace and for furthering the reunification of the German people.[211] Consequently, the *Osthandel* continued, trade was encouraged, and the Siberian Natural Gas Pipeline was completed in 1984, entirely as planned.

The years 1983, 1984 and 1985 saw the greatest levels of trade between the USSR and the FRG under Kohl's government.

---

208 Mastanduno, p. 271; Demidova, 'The Deal of the Century: The Reagan Administration and the Soviet Pipeline', p. 82.

209 'Harmal Report', NATO Archives <https://www.nato.int/cps/en/natohq/80830.htm>.

210 Bonn Government Declaration, 13 Oct. 1982, cited in BArch-Koblenz, B102/364337, Betr. 13. Tagung der deutsch-sowjetischen Wirtschaftskommission, 10 Sep. 1984, quoted in Carter, p. 153.

211 *The Harmel Report: Full Reports by the Rapporteurs on the Future Tasks of the Alliance*, 1967, NATO Archives <https://www.bits.de/NRANEU/nato-strategy/Harmel_Report_complete.pdf>; *Bonn Meeting*, 10 June 1982, NATO Archives <https://www.nato.int/docu/comm/49-95/c820610a.htm>.

Graph 12: West German import from and export to the USSR 1975-1989 in Mio DM.

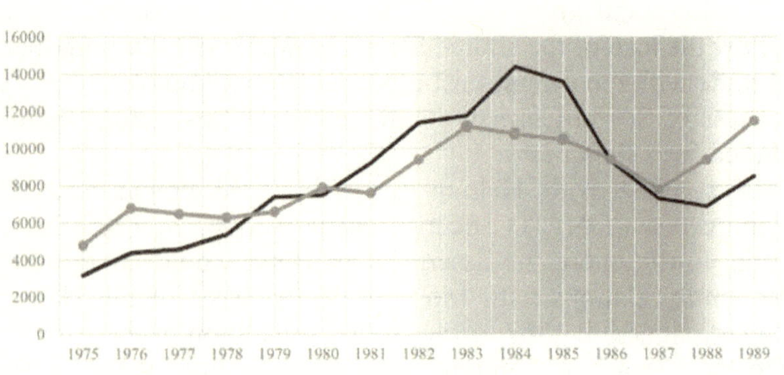

Source: Sensch, tbl. ZA8358.

It is important to note that the Soviets had achieved favourable balances. One possible reason for the high volume of trade in 1984 could be the beginning of Urengoy pipeline operations, which resulted in a significant quantity of purchased natural gas. It is also important to consider that the USSR was the leading producer of oil and natural gas in the mid-1980s, with a 34% share of global production for the latter. In particular, the Urangoy reserves demonstrated a notable increase in production, amounting to more than 200 bcm, over the five-year period spanning 1981 to 1985.[212]

---

212 BArch Koblenz, B 288/136, "Energiewirtschaft der UdSSR: Forcierte Erdgasförderung hat Erdölexporte stabilisiert", 19 August 1985, fols. 329-331

Graph 13: Natural Gas Imports per Suppliers in percentage rate 1982-1989

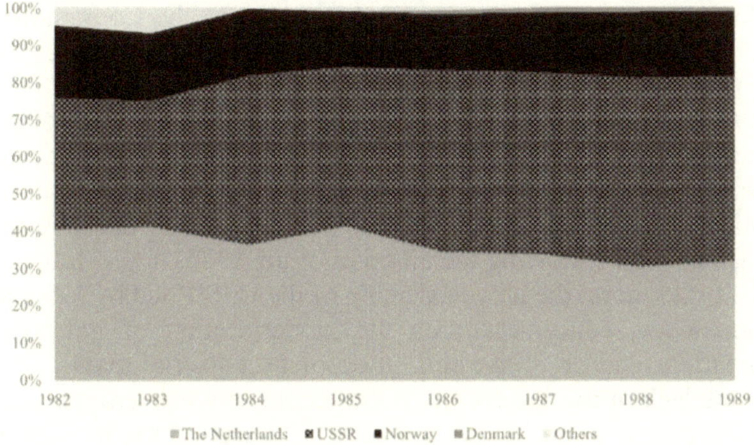

Source: 'Entwicklung des deutschen Gasmarktes
(monatliche Bilanz 1998 – 2017, Einfuhr seit 1960)'.

Concurrently, despite initial futile efforts, the USA did not impede West-East trade, thereby enabling the German government to expand commercial relations. However, internal issues within the USSR, including debt and currency exchange, constrained the possibility of new projects and limited western imports.[213]

A notable post-crisis event that demonstrated the continued willingness to pursue *Osthandel* was the meeting of the West German-Soviet Commission for Economic, Scientific and Technological Cooperation, which took place approximately five years after the crisis. This meeting was opened between the two parties on the basis of the 1970 treaty along with the development of the new Soviet five-year plan for the period 1986-1990, and opened new avenues for trade and cooperation between the FRG and Moscow. The new agreement secured the exchange of information, qualified personnel, experts, and scientific collaboration in several fields, including atomic

---

213 Rudolph, p. 336.

energy, energy technology, and space. Furthermore, the treaty established the Commission for Scientific and Technological Cooperation, which was required to report to the Commission for Economic, Scientific and Technological Cooperation on its activities.[214]

Concurrently, the USSR was experiencing a dearth of robust currency, as a consequence of the escalation in the price of petroleum and the expansion of petroleum production in the Middle East. This intensified competition, which had already been a factor following the oil crisis of the 1970s. (See Table 3)

Furthermore, the new leadership of the USSR, led by Mikhail Gorbachev, concentrated on the modernisation of industrial apparatus and on reinvesting in obsolete industrial plants. Due to the lack of foreign currency, these manoeuvres were financed at the cost of small CMEA countries. This created a resistance in the countries and forced Moscow to reduce arms expenditures.[215]

In addition to the novel economic trends observed in the USSR, another challenge emerged that negatively impacted the FRG-USSR relationship. This challenge was the US Technical Embargo, which affected the importation of a range of products, including small computers, energy devices, chips, and telephone switching systems. Notably, these products were the first to be included on the new CoCom embargo lists.[216]

Furthermore, it is important to note that in 1986, the USSR was significantly impacted by the nuclear disaster of Chernobyl, which undoubtedly had a profound effect on all aspects of Soviet economic activity. In this context, German industry, which had traditionally focused its relations with the East on economic matters and consistently sought to maintain a distance from political considerations, began to engage more actively on foreign policy issues and on mutual pacific aims. For example,

---

214 BArch-Koblenz, B 288/665, Abkommen zwischen der Regierung der Bundesrepublik Deutschland und der Regierung der Union der Sozialistischen Sowjetrepubliken über wissenschaftlich-technische Zusammenarbeit, 22 July 1986.
215 Rudolph, p. 338.
216 Mastanduno, p. 276; Wörmann, xxxviii, pp. 179–80.

between 1987 and 1988, German and Soviet businessmen and academics signed agreements on a number of themes, including cooperation for the protection of the environment, cooperation on exploration and use of space for peaceful purposes, and cooperation for the development of high-temperature reactors. In addition to this treaty, representatives of the *Ost-Ausschuss*, an industrial German organisation, offered their assistance to the Soviets in the training of export managers. However, this measure was also proved to be ineffective.[217] In addition, Deutsche Bank began to provide export credits in support of Gorbachev's policy, with the intention of restoring the Soviet economy and increasing the German-Soviet commercial balance. Despite being aware of the impending collapse of the Soviet economy, West Germany continued to finance the USSR for a fundamental reason: the hope that Moscow would approve German reunification. Consequently, German economic openness towards Moscow proved to be a profitable strategy in political terms at the end of Communism, despite the lack of tangible economic benefits.[218]

217 Jüngerkes, pp. 264–65.
218 Rudolph, pp. 339–41.

CONCLUSION

The subject of this book was the birth and development of the FRG's energy trade relations with the Soviet Union. It examined how and when the exchange of energy sources and equipment of energy industry between the two states arose and developed, and how and how much it was influenced by domestic and international political dynamics. In this analysis, the supra-state and superpower decision-making levels were considered, as well as the domestic level and the role of national companies. Upon completion of the analysis, it can be confirmed that Germany's long-standing energy dependence on Russia has its roots in the 1950s, when the first relations were established. The long-term analysis also shows that the perception of the importance of energy sources and their role on the European chessboard for the balance of the Western powers was not always consistent, or rather, not always in the foreground. The fact that the American leaders were not fully aware of this perception negatively impacted relations during a period when energy was a primary concern for Europeans. Indeed, despite the European allies' necessity for support, the USA found itself often in conflict with the other European countries, thereby marking a radical distancing, which also facilitated the increasingly consolidated relationship with the Eastern Bloc and the USSR in particular.

It is noteworthy that the energy sector was not the initial area of German-Russian collaboration. Rather, trade relations between the two countries have a longer history, dating back to the end of Nineteenth century and also in the first decades of the Twentieth century.[1] Despite experiencing crises, Weimar Germany and Nazi Germany between the wars managed to develop a flourishing trade with the Soviet Union. At the time, the energy component was not a significant concern, given that the European energy sector was heavily reliant on coal, a resource that was abundant in Germany.[2] In the aftermath of the Second World War, the formation of the Federal Republic of Germany, and then of the GDR, was intended to prevent a recurrence of the catastrophes of the early 1900s. However, the ideological opposition between the two blocs that emerged at the time became increasingly pronounced, and it even influenced trade between the parties.[3] The awareness of the importance of the restauration of German-Russian trade route for the restauration of the German economic apparatus was consistently evident in this context, not for the government, but rather for entrepreneurs, who started playing a pivotal role in newly establishing a trade relationship that subsequently became a significant aspect of the German-Western trade balance.

During the Cold War, energy sources and energy-related industrial goods were not only primarily economic goods but also diplomatic instruments. This was perceived both by the parties involved in the treaties and by other players on the international chessboard. The two actors, Bonn and Moscow – actually, the governments – began considering and utilising energy agreements to maintain diplomatic relations and to enhance their economic resilience and bargaining power in the global market.

The specific tendency of West Germany to regard the energy trade as the most sensitive and crucial aspect of both the trade balance with Moscow and as a key element in the elaboration of

---

1   Werner   Beitel   and   Jürgen   Nötzold,   *Deutsch-Sowjetische Wirtschaftsbeziehungen in Der Zeit Der Weimarer Republik,* Internationale Politik Und Sicherheit, 3 (Baden-Baden: Nomos Verlagsgesellschaft, 1979), p. 51.

2   Beitel and Nötzold, p. 76.

3   Sorokin; Wörmann, xxxviii; Daniel S. Hamilton, 'The Carrot and the Stick: German and American Approaches to East-West Trade, 1945-1985' (ProQuest Dissertations Publishing, 1985); Stent.

an internal energy security plan for the FRG and for a relaxed balance between the blocs that would ensure the 'warming' of tensions on European soil developed particularly during the last 30 years of the Cold War, and then consolidated and claimed a leading role in international negotiations during the last 20 years, when the discourse on energy diversification broadened to encompass not only oil but also natural and liquefied gas, and these resources, abundant in the USSR, became subjects of negotiation and trade. Especially in the two decades following the Moscow Treaty of 1970, this coincided with a development of West-German political and economic autonomy from the guidelines of the USA. It was evidenced by the establishment of a more enterprising trade, including energy trade, and cooperation with the East. One of the priorities of West Germany's economic policy at the time was, actually, to create more favourable conditions for the growth of German industries and its own growth as a power on the European stage and in the world market, also using flourishing trade with strategic partners. The USSR was one of these partners, since it was also the main supplier of primary energy sources Bonn could rely on, being one of the largest producers of fuels, including crude oil and natural gas. Indeed, it was during this period that the Soviet Union and Western states, including Italy, France and West Germany, engaged in intense negotiations concerning the potential exploitation of natural gas, despite various representations from the United States.

In general, rather than focusing on the political and strategic aspects of the energy trade between Moscow and Bonn, which is common in studies of the Cold War détente period between the blocs, and which also emerges in this study, it was emphasised its economic and commercial importance. This was crucial both for the West-German energy sector itself and thus for issues of energy security and transition, and for all related branches of trade in goods that were crucial for German industrial production. The chronological development of energy policy and the increase in energy negotiations is in perfect alignment with the domestic needs of the FRG to diversify energy sources in order to sustain domestic demand following crises. Additionally, it coincided with a significant shift in the political landscape at the highest levels of government, with the SPD becoming increasingly aligned with the Communist bloc and recognizing the pivotal role of trade as a key component in the larger plan for German reunification through détente and the importance of the industrial sector and industrial companies as a crucial factor in this process. It could also be observed, therefore, that the fundamental and primary economic element in West Germany's strategic energy relations with the East was evident in every state government, even when the diplomatic aspect was usually emphasised by the Chancellors themselves.

The advent of the Adenauer era marked a pivotal moment in the history of energy sources, particularly crude oil, which began to assume a pivotal role in global affairs. Despite the crisis of the late 1950s, coal remained the primary domestic source. Under his government, East Germany became one of the largest importers of oil from the USSR from the early 1960s, second only to Italy. This trade was connected to the one that had the opposite direction – from West to East – of large pipes: a sector that had been strongly promoted in recent years by entrepreneurs themselves, rather than by politicians, with the purely economic aim of being able to exploit the advantages of an interchange with the Soviet market and which aspired to restore important trade flows.

With Willi Brandt, the economic and business component was also recognised and exploited by the government, not so much because of the historical economic importance of the route for Germany and the Russian energy resources – at that time including natural gas – for the West German system, but rather because of the importance of political détente that trade agreements and related political arrangements could have for coexistence and international recognition. He and Bahr employed energy diplomacy to foster a relaxed international environment and to pave the way for a future agreement on the FRG question between Moscow and Bonn. The opening of the government, however, coincided with a sharp increase in trade and negotiations, marking the first half of the 1970s as a period of intense debate and planning for future interchanges.

In power, Schmidt, who had previously followed Brandt's policies, continued along the same lines. Unlike his predecessor, however, Schmidt had to deal with the effects of two energy shocks and the crisis of the Fordist-Keynesian regime. In such a context, the strategic and advantageous (in terms of energy security, proximity of sources and political security) component of the use of Soviet oil and gas certainly became more important than before. The sales and financing mechanism established between German pipe manufacturers and Soviet suppliers of raw materials was also consolidated, giving German companies a leading position not only on the domestic but also on the European market and making them the point of reference in Europe for all other Western partners vis-à-vis with the USSR.

In contrast to Adenauer, Brandt and Schmidt viewed the West Germany-Soviet energy trade as a "move left" that would firstly benefit German energy security strategy, primary objective of German energy policy following the initial energy crisis and the challenges in the European deposits too, and also enhance the FRG's independence from the USA. Schmidt also consolidated a clear contrast between the American ally and West Germany, as well as Europe as a whole. American policies in the 1970s and 1980s seemed increasingly divorced from European dynamics and blind to the welfare of its allies. This tendency, which was strong under Carter and even more so under Reagan, did nothing but move Europe and Germany towards other markets, and these, with a left-wing leadership attentive to both political and above all economic needs, were able to prioritise their own internal needs, especially regarding energy and trade.

Upon assuming power, Helmut Kohl too recognized the pivotal role of this trade for German economy and of West Germany within the European context. Even those with historically adversarial political orientations towards the USSR, including the most conservative elements, were now willing to continue the constructive trade relationship with the United States, rather than pursuing an unconditional alignment with American interests, that did nothing but damage German and European own economic sector, as well as the Soviet one.

Throughout this thesis, companies and the work of German banks in this context emerged as crucial actors. Especially German companies played a pivotal role in the establishment, implementation and perpetuation of West German-Soviet trade relations. In fact, the energy trade created new business opportunities for German steel and iron industries, for major companies such as Mannesmann AG, which provided equipment for the construction of energy infrastructures in Russia, Ruhrgas or Thyssengas. As already mentioned, the German government took a varied approach towards them. During the 1950s and 1960s, German industry representatives were largely absent from the political sphere and lacked an official voice in trade policy decision-making. Nevertheless, they have consistently espoused the value of West-East trade, particularly with regard to the exchange of energy resources via pipelines and related equipment between Bonn and Moscow. They always regarded this exchange as a pivotal sector of the German economy, and initially conducted the negotiations on a private corporative basis. However, following Brandt's ascension to power, this relationship shifted, with businessmen assuming a more active role in the national economic decision-making process. The establishment of several commissions during this period facilitated the process. German banks and credit insurance companies played a pivotal role in the negotiations conducted by European companies and the Soviet Union with regard to the construction of pipelines from the USSR to Europe. They facilitated the financing of the projects through the provision of long-term loans, which enabled the Soviet Union to address its shortage of hard currency, to accumulate foreign currency to settle outstanding payments to German industries, and, in doing so, to make trade possible.

TABLES

Table 1: FRG Export to USSR by commodities 1962-1968

	1962	1963	1964	1965	1966	1967	1968
General Export (Mio $)	207	154	194	147	135	198	273
Iron and steel (Mio $)	99.9	32.5	15.9	16.6	7.5	41	54.3
of which: large-diameter pipes (Mio $)	42.7	3.4	0.8	0.1	-	-	14.9
Balance of payments (Mio Mark)*	- 35	- 221	- 163	- 515	- 612	- 308	- 81

*Source: Sensch, tbl. ZA835. Other Source: Gesamtexport, Eisen und Stahl and Großrohre quoted by Wörmann, p.33. Data elaborated by author.

Table 2: Delivering of goods between the FRG and the USSR – in Mio DM

Year	Total Volume	German Imports	German Exports	Saldo
1960	1450.6	672.5	778.1	+105.6
1965	1686,8	1100.6	586.2	-514.4
1966	1694.3	1153	541,3	-611.7
1967	1891.9	1099.8	792.1	-307.7
1968	2269	1175.3	1093.7	-81.6
1969	2887.9	1305.7	1582.2	2765
1970	2800	1253.5	1546.5	293
1971	2885.1	1277.2	1607.9	330.7
1972	3681	1386.3	2295.4	909.1

Source: BArch-Koblenz, B 102/ 257471, Note about the development of
German-Soviet economic relations, Bonn, 26 September 1973

Table 3: Natural Gas production - NG in billion cubic metres

	Average DE Import Price (US dollars per million Btu)	USSR.[ ]	Russia	Saudi Arabia
1984	4	587.4	n/a	17.3
1985	4.25	642.9	424,9	17.9
1986	3.93	686.1	462.6	23.9
1987	2.55	727.4	500,5	25.5
1988	2.22	770	542.4	27.6
1989	2	796	566.3	28.3

Source.[1]: Soviet Energy Data Resource Handbook, p. 25. Other Source: 'Statistical Review of World Energy - All Data, 1965-2017' (BP, 2018) <https://nangs.org/analytics/bp-statistical-review-of-world-energy-2018-edition-pdf-xlsx> [last accessed 20 May 2024].

BIBLIOGRAPHY

Archival sources

Federal German Archives, Koblenz (BArch Koblenz)
    Ministry of Economy (B 102)
    Office of the Federal Precidency (B 122)
    Chancellor's Office (B 136)
    Permanent Representation of the Federal Republic of Germany to the German Democratic Republic (B 288)
Federal German Archives, Berlin-Lichterfelde (BArch Berlin-Lichterfelde)
    Ministerium für Außenhandel und Innendeutschen Handel (DL 2)
    Bereich Kommerzielle Koordinierung (DL 226)
Political Archive of the German Foreign Office, Online Database (PA AA)
    Büro Staatssekretäre (B-2-B STS)
    Sowjetunion (B 41-REF)
    Edition "Akten zur Auswärtigen Politik der Bundesrepublik Deutschland" (B 150-AAPD)
    Büro Reichsminister (RZ 101)
Stasi Unterlagen Archiv, Berlin (BStU)
    Volkswirtschaft - Hauptabteilungen XVIII (HA XVIII)

Books

Abelshauser, Werner, *Deutsche Wirtschaftsgeschichte. Von 1945 bis zur Gegenwart* (München: C.H.Beck, 2004)

Adomeit, Hannes, *Imperial Overstretch. Germany in Soviet Policy from Stalin to Gorbachev*, 2° (Baden-Baden: Nomos, 2016)

Balmaceda, Margarita Mercedes, *Russian Energy Chains: The Remaking of Technopolitics from Siberia to Ukraine to the European Union*, Woodrow Wilson Center Press Series (New York: Columbia University Press, 2021) <https://doi.org/10.7312/balm19748>

Beitel, Werner, and Jürgen Nötzold, *Deutsch-Sowjetische Wirtschaftsbeziehungen in Der Zeit Der Weimarer Republik*, Internationale

Politik Und Sicherheit, 3 (Baden-Baden: Nomos Verlagsgesellschaft, 1979)

Bini, Elisabetta, Giuliano Garavini, and Federico Romero, eds., *Oil Shock. The 1973 Crisis and Its Economic Legacy* (London/New York: I.B. Tauris, 2016)

Blom, Frank, *Beschaffungsmarktforschung* (Wiesbaden: Gabler, 1982)

Bros, Aurélie, Tatiana Mitrova, and Kirsen Westphal, *German-Russian Gas Relations – A Special Relationship in Troubled Waters* (Berlin: SWP Research Paperà, 2017)

Caciagli, Federica, *La Germania Est tra Mosca e Bonn. Ostpolitik e Westpolitik nel Rilancio del Processo di Sicurezza in Europa.1969-1975* (Roma: Carocci, 2010)

Campanini, Massimo, *Storia Del Medio Oriente Contemporaneo*, VI (Bologna: Il Mulino, 2006)

Carter, Charles William, *The Importance of Osthandel: West German-Soviet Trade and the End of the Cold War, 1969-1991* (The Ohio State University, 2012) <https://etd.ohiolink.edu/acprod/odb_etd/ws/send_file/send?accessi on=osu1346850432&disposition=inline>

Corni, Gustavo, *Storia della Germania. Da Bismarck a Merkel* (Milano: Il Saggiatore, 1995)

Di Nolfo, Ennio, *Storia delle Relazioni Internazionali II – Gli anni della Guerra Fredda 1946-1990* (Roma-Bari: Laterza, 2008)

Fink, Carole, Axel Frohn, and Jürgen Heideking, *Genoa, Rapallo, and European Reconstruction in 1922, Genoa, Rapallo, and European Reconstruction in 1922*, Publications of the German Historical Institute (Cambridge: Cambridge University Press, 1991)

Goldman, Marshall I., *Petrostate: Putin, Power, and the New Russia* (New York: Oxford University Press, 2010)

Gross, Stephen G., *Energy and Power: Germany in the Age of Oil, Atoms, and Climate Change*, Online edn (New York: Oxford University Press, 2023)

Grossfeld, Bernhard, and Abbo Junker, *Das CoCom im Internationalen Wirtschaftsrecht, Das CoCom im Internationalen Wirtschaftsrecht UniMi* (Tubingen: J.C.B. Mohr, 1991)

Hildebrand, Klaus, *Das Vergangene Reich, Deutsche Außenpolitik von Bismarck Bis Hitler 1871-1945*. Studienausgabe (Oldenbourg Wissenschaftsverlag, 2008) <https://doi.org/10.1524/9783486719352>

Högselius, Per, *Red Gas: Russia and the Origins of European Energy Dependence* (New York: Palgrave Macmillan, 2013)

Jope, Alfred, *Erdöl und Erdgas als wirtschaftliche und politische Faktoren* (Frankfurt a.M: Hirschgraben, 1976)

Jüngerkes, Sven, *Diplomaten der Wirtschaft. Die Geschichte des Ost-Ausschusses der Deutschen Wirtschaft* (Osnabrück: Fibre, 2012)

Karlsch, Rainer, and Raymond G. Stokes, *Faktor Öl. Die Mineralölwirtschaft in Deutschland 1859-1974* (München: C.H. Beck, 2003)

Mastanduno, Michael, *Economic Containment: Cocom and the Politics of East-West Trade*, Cornell Studies in Political Economy (Ithaca, NY: Cornell University Press, 2019)

Maugeri, Leonardo, *L'era del petrolio: mitologia, storia e futuro della più controversa risorsa del mondo*, trans. by Alessandro Maugeri, *L'era del petrolio : mitologia, storia e futuro della più controversa risorsa del mondo*, Serie bianca (Milano: Feltrinelli, 2006)

Rudolph, Karsten, *Wirtschaftsdiplomatie im Kalten Krieg. Die Ostpolitik der westdeutschen Großindustrie 1945-1991* (Frankfurt a.M./New York: Campus, 2004)

Salzmann, Stephanie C., *Great Britain, Germany and the Soviet Union: Rapallo and after, 1922-1934*, Royal Historical Society Studies in History New (London: Boydell, 2002)

Schmidt, Helmut, *Uomini al Potere* (Milano: Sugarco, 1987)

Sodaro, Michael J., *Moscow, Germany, and the West from Khrushev to Gorbachev* (London: I.B. Tauris, 1991)

Spicka, Mark E., *Selling the Economic Miracle: Economic Reconstruction and Politics in West Germany, 1949-1957*, Monographs in German History (New York: Berghahn Books, 2007), xviii

Spohr, Kristina, *The Global Chancellor - Helmut Schmidt and the Reshaping of the International Order* (Oxford: Oxford University Press, 2016)

Stent, Angela, *From Embargo to Ostpolitik. The Political Economy of West German-Soviet Relations, 1955-1980* (Cambridge: Cambridge University Press, 1981)

Torp, Cornelius, *The Challenges of Globalization*, Economy and Politics in Germany, 1860-1914 (Berghahn Books, 2014) <https://doi.org/10.1515/9781782385035>

Verda, Matteo, *Politica estera e sicurezza energetica. L'esperienza europea, il gas naturale e il ruolo della Russia* (Novi Ligure: Epoké, 2012)

Von Dannenberg, Julia, *The Foundations of Ostpolitik: The Making of the Moscow Treaty between West Germany and the USSR*, Oxford Historical Monographs (Oxford: Oxford University press, 2008)

Vonyó, Tamás, *The Economic Consequences of the War: West Germany's Growth Miracle after 1945*, Cambridge Studies in Economic History (Cambridge: Cambridge University Press, 2018)

Weber, Hermann, *Geschichte Der DDR* (München: Deutscher Taschenbuch Verlag, 1999)

Wörmann, Claudia, *Osthandel Als Problem Der Atlantischen Allianz. Erfahrung Aus Dem Erdgas-Röhren-Geschäft Mit Der UdSSR*, Arbeitspapiere zur Internationalen Politik (Bonn: Europa Union, 1986), xxxviii

Yergin, Daniel, *The Prize: The Epic Quest for Oil, Money & Power* (Simon and Schuster, 2011)

Chapters or Articles in Books

Bollard, Alan, 'A Continental Middle Way: Ludwig Erhard and Social Market Economists', in *Economists in the Cold War: How a Handful of Economists Fought the Battle of Ideas* (Oxford University Press, 2023) <https://doi.

org/10.1093/oso/9780192887399.003.0004>

Demidova, Ksenia, 'La Politica degli Stati Uniti nei confronti dell'influenza sovietica sull'Europa Occidentale, 1973-1985', in *La Fine Del Petrolio. Risorse Energetiche e Democrazia Nell'età Contemporanea*, by Elisabetta Bini and Simone Selva (Napoli: L'ancora del Mediterraneo, 2011), pp. 111-131

―――, 'The Deal of the Century: The Reagan Administration and the Soviet Pipeline', in *European Integration and the Atlantic Community in the 1980s*, ed. by Kiran Klaus Patel and KennethEditors Weisbrode (Cambridge University Press, 2013), pp. 59–82

Engels, Markus, and Petra Schwartz, 'Alliierte Restriktionen Für Die Außenwirtschaftspolitik Der Bundesrepublik Deutschland. Das Röhrenembargo von 1962/63 Und Das Erdgas-Röhren-Geschäft von 1982', in *"...die volle Macht eines souveränen Staates...". Die Alliierten Vorbehaltsrechte als Rahmenbedingung westdeutscher Außenpolitik 1949-1990*, by Helga Haftendorn and Henning Riecke (Baden-Baden: Berlin-Brandenburgische Akademie der Wissenschaften,1996), pp. 227-242 <https://edoc.bbaw.de/frontdoor/index/index/year/2007/docId/362>

Farrenkopf, Michael, 'Short-Term Rise and Decades of Decline: German Hard Coal Mining after 1945', in *Boom - Crisis - Heritage: King Coal and the Energy Revolutions after 1945*, ed. by Lars Bluma, Michael Farrenkopf, and Torsten Meyer (Berlin, Boston: De Gruyter Oldenbourg, 2021), pp. 131–46 <https://doi.org/doi:10.1515/9783110729948-010>

Kieninger, Stephan, 'Between Power Politics and Morality', in *The Long Détente: Changing Concepts of Security and Cooperation in Europe, 1950s–1980s*, ed. by Oliver Bange and Poul Villaume (Central European University Press, 2017), pp. 281–314 <https://doi.org/10.1515/9789633861295-014>

Kosthorst, Daniel, 'Primat Der Politik Als Primat Der Bündnispolitik: Zum Streit Um Das Röhrenembargo Gegen Die UdSSR', in *Studien Zur Auswärtigen Politik Der Bundesrepublik Deutschland 1963*, ed. by Rainer Blasius (Berlin, Boston: Oldenbourg Wissenschaftsverlag, 1994), pp. 97–117 <https://doi.org/doi:10.1524/9783486703092-004>

La Barca, Giuseppe, 'The Oil Shock, the Partial Recovery and Their Impact on Trade Policies Across the Atlantic', in *The US, the EC and World Trade: From the Kennedy Round to the Start of the Uruguay Round* (London: Bloomsbury Academic, 2016)

Lippert, Werner D., 'European Long-Term Investments in Détente', in *The Long Détente: Changing Concepts of Security and Cooperation in Europe, 1950s–1980s*, ed. by Oliver Bange and Poul Villaume (Central European University Press, 2017), pp. 77–94 <https://doi.org/10.1515/9789633861295-006>

―――, 'The Economics of "Ostpolitik": West Germany, the United States, and the Gas Pipeline Deal', in *The Strained Alliance. U.S. - European Relations from Nixon to Carter*, ed. by Matthias Schulz and Thomas A. Schwartz (Cambridge: Cambridge University Press, 2010), pp. 65–81

Articles in Journals

Belov, Vladivoslav B., 'A Paradigm Change in Energy Cooperation between Germany and Russia', *Herald of the Russian Academy of Sciences*, 92.Suppl 6 (2022), 512–20 <https://doi.org/10.1134/S1019331622120024>

Berghahn, Volker R., 'Ordoliberalism, Ludwig Erhard and West Germany's "Economic Basic Law"', *European Review of International Studies*, 2.3 (2015), 37–47

Fleischhauer, Eva Ingeborg, 'Rathenau in Rapallo: Eine notwendige Korrektur des Forschungsstandes', *Vierteljahrshefte für Zeitgeschichte*, 54.3 (2006), 365–415

Glazer, Stephen G., 'The Brezhnev Doctrine', *The International Lawyer*, 5.1 (1971), 169–79

Graf, Rüdiger, 'Making Use of the "Oil Weapon": Western Industrialized Countries and Arab Petropolitics', *Diplomatic History*, 36.1 (2012), 185–208

Gross, Stephen G., 'Making Space for Sanctions: The Economics of German Natural Gas Imports from Russia, 1982 and 2014 Compared', *German Politics and Society*, 34.3 (2016), 1–25

——, 'The German Economy and East-Central Europe: The Development of Intra-Industry Trade from Ostpolitik to the Present"', *German Politics and Society*, 31.3 (2013), 83–105 <https://doi.org/10.3167/gps.2013.310305>

Kieninger, Stephan, 'Diplomacy beyond Deterrence: Helmut Schmidt and the Economic Dimension of Ostpolitik', *Cold War History*, 20.2 (2020), 179–96

Maliszewska-Nienartowicz, Justyna, 'Impact of Russia's Invasion of Ukraine on Renewable Energy Development in Germany and Italy', *Utilities Policy*, 87 (2024) <https://doi.org/10.1016/j.jup.2024.101731>

Melsted, Odinn, and Irene Pallua, 'The Historical Transition from Coal to Hydrocarbons: Previous Explanations and the Need for an Integrative Perspective', *Canadian Journal of History*, 53.3 (2018) <https://www.utpjournals.press/doi/full/10.3138/cjh.ach.53.3.03>

Rustow, Dankwart A., 'Who Won the Yom Kippur and Oil Wars?', *Foreign Policy*, 17, 1974, 166–75 <https://doi.org/10.2307/1148119>

Schlarp, Karl-Heinz, 'Das Dilemma des Westdeutschen Osthandels und die Entstehung des Ost-Ausschusses der Deutschen Wirtschaft 1950-1952', *Vierteljahrshefte Für Zeitgeschichte*, 2 (1993), 223–76

Sorokin, Aleksey, 'The Soviet Union's Economic Relations with Austria and the Federal Republic of Germany: Political Factors and the Art of Diplomacy (1955-1964)', *Quaestio Rossica*, 10.5 (2022), 1657–73 <https://doi.org/10.15826/qr.2022.5.753>

von Strandmann, Harmut Pogge, 'Grossindustrie Und Rapallopolitik: Deutsch-Sowjetische Handelsbeziehungen in Der Weimarer Republik', *Historische Zeitschrift*, 222.1 (1976), 265–341 <https://doi.org/10.1524/hzhz.1976.222.jg.265>

Yergin, Daniel, 'Politics and Soviet-American Trade: The Three Questions', *Foreign Affairs*, 55.3 (1977), 517–38 <https://doi.org/10.2307/20039684>

Articles in Newspaper

'Bonn Bids U.S. Halt Arms to Israel via Germany', *New York Times*, 1973, 20

Kemezis, Paul, 'West German Trade Surplus Set a Record in 1974', *New York Times*, 30 January 1975 <https://www.nytimes.com/1975/01/30/archives/west-german-trade-surplus-set-a-record-in-1974.html>

Nagel, Walter, 'Gibst Du Röhren - Geb' Ich Gas', *Die Zeit*, 19 December 1969, 51 edition <https://www.zeit.de/1969/51/gibst-du-roehren-geb-ich-gas/seite-2>

Zundel, Rudolf, 'Das Ende Der Doktrin?', *Die Zeit*, 6 June 1969, 23–24 edition, pp. 7–8

Published documents

'Address given by Willy Brandt on the Basic Treaty (Bonn, 15 February 1973)', in *Verhandlungen Des Deutschen Bundestages.*, 81, 14 vols (Bonn: Deutscher Bundestag und Bundesrat, 1972), pp. 534–38 <https://www.cvce.eu/en/obj/address_given_by_willy_brandt_on_the_basic_treaty_bonn_15_february_1973-en-0154bfcf-07a4-4c97-9ef0-967526b35381.html>

'Agreement Between the Allied High Commission in Germany and the West German Federal Republic, Signed at Bonn, November 24, 1949', *International Organization*, 4.1 (1950), 184–87

'Agreement between the United States and the Soviet Union on Measures for Reducing the Risk of Outbreak of Nuclear War (Washington, September 30, 1971)', in *Western European Union Assembly-General Affairs Committee: A Retrospective View of the Political Year in Europe 1971* (Paris: Western European Union Assembly - General Affairs Committee, 1972) <https://www.cvce.eu/en/obj/agreement_between_the_united_states_and_the_soviet_union_on_measures_for_reducing_the_risk_of_outbreak_of_nuclear_war_washington_30_september_1971-en-fd9101b8-15c7-494c-a763-a384c58fa394.html>

Bahr, Egon, 'Wandel Durch Annährung. Ein Diskussionsbeitrag in Tutzing. (Redemanuskript)', 1963, Archiv der sozialen Demokratie der Friedrich-Ebert-Stiftung, Bonn <https://www.1000dokumente.de/index.html?c=dokument_de&dokument=0091_bah&object=facsimile&pimage=1&v=100&nav=&l=de>

Bonn Meeting, 10 June 1982, NATO Archives <https://www.nato.int/docu/comm/49-95/c820610a.htm>

Brandt, Willy, *My Life in Politic* (London: Hamish Hamilton Ltd, 1992) <http://www.cvce.eu/obj/willy_brandt_my_life_in_politics-en-a21dae1a-a392-44c3-9cfd-2017525d1c32.html>

Doeker, Günther, and Jens A. Brückner, eds., *The Federal Republic of Germany, and the German Democratic Republic in International Relations. Vol. I: Confrontation and Cooperation* (Dobbs Ferry, NY: Oceana Publications, Inc., 1979), i

'Erklärung von Helmut Schmidt (Helsinki, 30. Juli 1975)', in *Bulletin Des Presse- Und Informationsamtes Der Bundesregierung*, 98, Presse-und Informationsamt der Bundesregierung (Bonn: Deutscher Bundesverlag, 1975)

Freiberg, Phillip, 'Reagan Administration and the Soviet Pipeline Embargo', 2011 <https://doi.org/10.13140/2.1.1340.0964>

Hamilton, Daniel S., 'The Carrot and the Stick: German and American Approaches to East-West Trade, 1945-1985' (ProQuest Dissertations Publishing, 1985)

'Harmal Report', NATO Archives <https://www.nato.int/cps/en/natohq/80830.htm>

'Helsinki Decalogue (1 August 1975)', in *OSCE. Documens 1973-1997* (Vienna: Organization for Security and Cooperation in Europe) <https://www.cvce.eu/obj/helsinki_decalogue_1_august_1975-en-1bccd494-0f57-4816-ad18-6aaba4d73d56.html>

'International Trade Statistics 1900-1960' (United Nations Statistics Division (UNSD), 1962) <https://unstats.un.org/unsd/trade/imts/Historical%20data%201900-1960.pdf> [last accessed 24 May 2024]

Luns, Joseph, 'NATO Council, Rome 4th-5th May, 1981. Final Communiqué.', NATO Online Library <https://www.nato.int/docu/comm/49-95/c810504a.htm>

'News Conference Remarks by Chairman Ulbricht on Negotiation of a Treaty Establishing Equal Relations Between East and West Germany, January 19, 1970', in *United States-Department of State. Documents on Germany 1944-1985*, Department of State Publication, 9446 (Washington: Department of State, 1970), pp. 1065–67 <https://www.cvce.eu/obj/press_conference_by_walter_ulbricht_19_january_1970-en-413e904a-5a45-4a6b-97d4-cc259bd87efe.html>

'Protocol of the Agreements Reached between the Allied High Commissioners and the Chancellor of the German Federal Republic at the Petersberg (November 22, 1949)', in *Documents on Germany under Occupation* (London/New York: Oxford University Press, 1955), pp. 439–42 <https://germanhistorydocs.ghi-dc.org/pdf/eng/Founding%208%20ENG.pdf> [last accessed 24 May 2024]

Reconciliation of Soviet and Western Foreign Trade Statistics (Washington: Central Intelligence Agency, May 1977), General CIA Records <https://www.cia.gov/readingroom/docs/CIA-RDP08S01350R000602080001-1.pdf>

Scheel, Walter. Letter to Andrej Gromyko, 'Brief zur deutschen Einheit', 12 August 1970 <https://www.chronik-der-mauer.de/material/180318/brief-zur-deutschen-einheit-12-august-1970>

'Soviet Commentary on the Quadripartite Agreement', in *United States-Department of State. Documents on Germany 1944-1985* (Washington: Department of State Publication, 1971), pp. 1153–54 <https://www.cvce.eu/obj/soviet_commentary_on_the_quadripartite_agreement_4_september_1971-en-9ffbda8b-c2a1-4aa2-a7a1-5ceec8302be4.html>

The Harmel Report: Full Reports by the Rapporteurs on the Future Tasks of the Alliance, 1967, NATO Archives <https://www.bits.de/NRANEU/nato-strategy/Harmel_Report_complete.pdf>

'The Moscow Treaty (12 Aug. 1970)', in *United States-Department of State. Documents on Germany 1944-1985* (Washington: Department of State Publication), pp. 1103–5 <https://www.cvce.eu/obj/the_moscow_treaty_12_august_1970-en-d5341cb5-1a49-4603-aec9-0d2304c25080.html>

'The Quadripartite Agreement on Berlin (3 Sept. 1971)', in *Documents on Germany 1944-1985*, Department of State Publication 9446 (Washington: Department of State), pp. 1135–43 <https://www.cvce.eu/obj/quadripartite_agreement_on_berlin_berlin_3_september_1971-en-9bfcb5f5-8e0d-46ee-9f7f-8e9a7c945fa7.html>

The Soviet Gas Pipeline in Perspective (Directorate of Intelligence, 17 September 1982) <https://www.cia.gov/readingroom/document/cia-rdp88b00443r001203970095-9>

"Western Europe: Economic Links with the Soviet Bloc". An Intelligence Assessment (Directorate of Intelligence, 1 May 1983), p. 31, General CIA Records <https://www.cia.gov/readingroom/docs/CIA-RDP84S00555R000200050003-4.pdf>

Dataset and Handbooks

'Entwicklung des deutschen Gasmarktes (monatliche Bilanz 1998 – 2017, Einfuhr seit 1960)' (BAFA) <https://www.bafa.de/SharedDocs/Downloads/DE/Energie/egas_entwicklung_1991.html>

Höpfner, Bernd, 'Der Deutsche Außenhandel 1900 – 1945.', 2011, Published: GESIS Datenarchiv, Köln. ZA8469 Datenfile Version 1.0.0, <https://doi.org/10.4232/1.10317>

Impact of Oil Exports from the Soviet Bloc (Washington, DC: National Petroleum Council, 1964) <https://www.energy.gov/sites/default/files/2022-11/1964-Impact_of_Oil_Exports_from_Soviet_Bloc-Supplement.pdf>

Rahlf, Thomas, *Deutschland in Daten. Zeitreihen Zur Historischen Statistik* (Bonn: Bundeszentrale für politische Bildung, 17 November 2022) <https://www.bpb.de/system/files/dokument_pdf/deutschland_in_daten_online_komplett.pdf>

Sensch, Jürgen, 'Der Außenhandel Deutschlands. Basisdaten Für Den Zeitraum 1830 Bis 2000', 2009 <https://doi.org/10.4232/1.8358>

Soviet Energy Data Resource Handbook, CIA Historical Review Program

(Directorate of Intelligence, May 1990), p. 25 <https://www.cia.gov/readingroom/document/0000292332>

Sowjetunion 1970, Allgemeine Statistik Des Auslandes / Länderkurzberichte (Stuttgart und Mainz: Statistisches Bundesamt, 1970) <https://www.statistischebibliothek.de/mir/receive/DEHeft_mods_00080421>

Sowjetunion 1977, Allgemeine Statistik des Auslandes / Länderkurzberichte (Stuttgart und Mainz: Statistisches Bundesamt, 1977) <https://www.destatis.de/GPStatistik/content/below/index.xml>

'Statistical Review of World Energy - All Data, 1965-2017' (BP, 2018) <https://nangs.org/analytics/bp-statistical-review-of-world-energy-2018-edition-pdf-xlsx> [last accessed 20 May 2024]

'Statistisches Jahrbuch für das Deutsche Reich', 1935 <https://www.digizeitschriften.de/id/514401303_1934|log1>

'————', 1940 <https://www.digizeitschriften.de/id/514401303_1939|log1>

'————', 1926 <https://www.digizeitschriften.de/id/514401303_1924|log1>

'————', 1928 <https://www.digizeitschriften.de/id/514401303_1927|log1>

'Statistisches Jahrbuch für die Bundesrepublik Deutschland', 1975 (1976) <https://www.digizeitschriften.de/id/514402342_1975|log1>

'Struktur des Energieverbrauchs' (AGEB - AG Energiebilanzen e.V., 2010), Zeitreihen bis 1989 <https://ag-energiebilanzen.de/daten-und-fakten/zeitreihen-bis-1989/>

Sitography

IEA: <https://www.iea.org/about/emergency-response-and-energy-security>

JEIA: <https://images.library.wisc.edu/History/EFacs/GerRecon/Bizonal/reference/history.bizonal.i0011.pdf>.

Osterroth, Franz, and Dieter Schuster, 'Stichtag 11./14. Mai 1970', in *Chronik Der Deutschen Sozialdemokratie* (Berlin: Electronic ed., 2001) <https://library.fes.de/fulltext/bibliothek/chronik/band3/e235g1652.html>

SALT: <https://history.state.gov/milestones/1969-1976/salt

Printed by
Rotomail Italia S.p.A.
June 2025